CW00369164

Hitlers
of
Liverpool

© Michael Unger 2011
Published by The Bluecoat Press, Liverpool
Book design by March Design, Liverpool
Printed by Martins the Printers, Berwick

ISBN 9781904438991

www.bluecoatpress.co.uk

The Hitlers of Liverpool

Michael Unger

THE BLUECOAT PRESS

INTRODUCTION

Adolf Hitler lived in Liverpool from November 1912 to April 1913, in order to avoid being called up in the Austrian army. His Irish sister-in-law Bridget Hitler makes this startling allegation in her unfinished memoir *My Brother-in-law Adolf*.

Bridget Elizabeth Dowling, through the accident of marriage, was related to one of the most notorious men of our time. In 1909, the 17-year-old Bridget had met Adolf Hitler's volatile half brother Alois in Dublin and fallen in love with him. The couple had then married in London against the wishes of her father. Some time in the 1940s, Bridget, by then living in America, wrote her memoirs, with the help of her Liverpool-born son William Patrick Hitler.

The existence of Bridget Hitler's memoirs has been known since the early 1970s, when the Canadian historian, Professor Alan Cassels, wrote to me at the *Liverpool Daily Post*, where I was then deputy editor, saying that he had just read the proofs of a new biography of Hitler by Robert Payne. Though he deemed the book a dreadful pot-boiler, he acknowledged that Payne had dug up one new and astonishing piece of evidence about Hitler's youth, in the form of an unpublished memoir, stretching to 220 pages, entitled *My Brother-in-law Adolf*. Professor Payne had read the memoirs in the Manuscript Division of the New York Public Library.

The account in the memoirs of Hitler's alleged visit to Liverpool in 1912, led, in the spring of 1973, to a lengthy series of articles in the *Liverpool Daily Post*. Since then a number of historians have referred to the memoirs, including Robert Waite in his study of Hitler, *The Psychopathic God* and Ian Kershaw in *Hitler 1889-1936*.

Cassels is a specialist on Second World War fascism and at the time was Professor of History at McMaster University, Hamilton, Ontario. He was born and brought up in Liverpool and was inclined to believe Bridget's account: "The Merseyside details are certainly circumstantially credible. Although Adolf Hitler never referred publicly or privately to a Liverpool visit," says Cassels, "I'm inclined to believe his sister-in-law. The young Adolf was on the run from the Austrian police for draft evasion at this time; in 1913 he fled to Munich to escape the Austrian authorities, so why not to England earlier?"

Although it is well known that, at the time, Adolf did not get on at all well with Alois, as Bridget affirms in her memoirs, Adolf persuaded his sister Angela to give him the money Alois had sent her and her husband to visit him in Liverpool. Apparently the Austrian authorities were close to arresting Adolf for draft evasion and he had to flee Vienna.

Six years after the publication of the *Daily Post* articles, in 1979, the memoirs were published in full for the first time in my book *The Memoirs of Bridget Hitler*. This edition of the book contains Bridget Hitler's memoirs as well as the story of Hitler's living American family. I have updated what happened to Bridget and William Patrick in the years leading up to the Second World War, and have included a new section on their family life in America.

The Liverpool Hitlers had emigrated to New York in 1939 where Bridget worked for the British Red Cross in

New York. William Patrick lectured about Adolf Hitler and the Nazis in both America and Canada, before joining the US Navy. He was honourably discharged after the war, when he married a young German woman he had fallen in love with in the 1930s. William Patrick and his bride moved to Long Island, along with Bridget, where they and their family lived for the rest of their lives.

Adolf Hitler during the First World War.

AMERICA

In the early November of 2004, Phyllis Stuart-Houston, aged 81, was buried in the Holy Sepulchre Roman Catholic Cemetery in Coram, Long Island, near New York. She joined the husband she called Willy and her mother-in-law Brigid (sic) in the three-person plot.

William Patrick had died some 17 years before in 1987 and his mother had died in 1969. Phyllis's son, Howard, who had died in a road accident in 1989, was buried nearby. The quiet, well maintained cemetery is only a few miles from their suburban homes in Patchogue. But Phyllis, who lived at home in Germany throughout the war, died with her secret intact – her husband was William Patrick Hitler and her mother-in-law, Bridget Elizabeth, was Adolf Hitler's sister-in-law, as a result of her marriage to Alois Hitler, his half brother.

However, the marble headstones merely report their changed surname of Stuart-Houston. 'Rest in Peace' is carved on the main grave and 'Always and Forever' above Howard's name on his grave.

The journey that ended in a suburban American cemetery had been a tortuous one for Irish-born Bridget and Liverpudlian William Patrick; a journey that had involved the Nuremberg rallies, William Patrick's arrest by the Nazis, Hitler's probable murder of his niece Geli and both the British and American secret services.

Although the story started at the Dublin Horse Show long before the First World War, the traumas began when Bridget's brother-in-law Adolf came to visit her and her

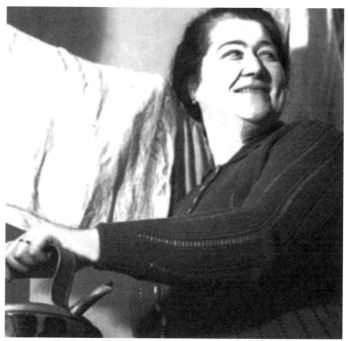

Bridget Hitler in America..

THE HOBO NEWS
TO HELL WITH HITLER
PUBLIC ENEMY N...

Bridget and William Patrick in New York.

Bridget in New York.

new family in Toxteth, Liverpool, in 1912. This eventually led to mother and son deciding to emigrate to America in 1939, after William Patrick had fled Germany fearing he was about to be exposed as a British spy and having been told by Adolf Hitler that he must become a German citizen.

On returning from Germany to his mother in England in early 1939, William Patrick had been hired by London literary agents, William Morris, to embark on a lecture tour of America, talking about his Uncle Adolf. And so, in February 1939, he and Bridget, filmed by *Pathe News* and their visitors' visas safely in their hands, set sail from Europe on the French liner *SS Normandie,* under the name of Carter Stevens. On arrival in New York on 30 March 1939, William Patrick Hitler readily acknowledged his real name and happily told waiting reporters: "In the event of war, I'll join up immediately."

Bridget and William Patrick briefly rented a house in the New York suburb of Jamaica and then stayed in a couple of New York hotels – the Buckingham (where he recovered from the 'flu) and the Concord. In June 1939 they moved into 505W 142nd Street, New York, their home until the end of the war.

Although he wanted to join up – or at least made a point of saying he did – William Patrick quickly started his lecture tours. He also gave many interviews, wrote for newspapers and magazines and, bizarrely, broadcast to South America on behalf of the US government.

As well as talking about "My Uncle Adolf", he also talked about life in contemporary Germany (where he had lived for many years) and the infamous Nazis he had met such as the 'sane' Hess. His lectures were similar in content to two articles he wrote at the time: 'Why I Hate My Uncle', was published in *Look* magazine in January 1939 and 'Mon Oncle Adolphe', was published in *Paris-Soir* the following August. For example, on 24 October 1939, in a talk in New York, he would 'present a startling story of the real Germany "hidden behind Nazi fictions", and five days later, also in New York, he talked about "What the German people are thinking today'. He charged the organisers a fee of about $150 for speaking, with the net proceeds from ticket sales, which could be around $300, being given to the British Red Cross. Bridget was mainly supported by William Patrick from the proceeds of his talks.

William Patrick soon went on an extensive tour of the States and Canada. In Toronto he said he was going to join the Canadian Army, but this was regarded by those who knew him as a publicity stunt, as he quickly qualified it by saying that the Canadian government "considers it more pertinent for him to continue his lectures".

Back in the US, though, things were not going quite to plan with his English agents, as they had expected him to attract larger audiences. This led to him being managed by agents William B Feakins Inc (of 500 Fifth Ave, New York). It also brought him more formally to the attention of the FBI, who had been keeping a close eye on him since soon after his arrival.

In 1941, William Patrick gave a talk, the flier for which said:

MEN! Hear!
HITLER
William Patrick
(nephew of Adolph)
Explain the Mystery
of Rudolph Hess
at
MEN'S LEAGUE
Marble Collegiate Church
1 West 39th St
November 11, 1941
dinner 6.30pm
Make Reservations To-day

This circular was passed on to the FBI "for its information".

Before long, William Patrick started to have his talks and fees questioned. In February 1942, when he gave a speech at the Sandley High School, Winchester, Virginia, his 'exorbitant' fee of $150 led to a complaint to the FBI on behalf of the Mayor of Winchester by Andrew Bell, secretary of the local Chamber of Commerce. As well as complaining about the fee, Bell also wanted to know what the FBI had on its files about William Patrick. Bell received a reply from the very top of the agency, with J Edgar Hoover saying that unless Bell had the permission of the Attorney-General, the FBI's files were strictly confidential – but if Bell heard "anything of interest to the protection of the nation's security" he should tell Hoover immediately.

Bell, however, seems not to have been satisfied with the reply, telling the Mayor in a note on Hoover's response, that in his speech at the school, William Patrick initially disapproved of his uncle's ideology, but towards the end of the speech caused anger among his audience by saying that the German people weren't all that bad.

Despite its reluctance to help Bell, the FBI, a few weeks later, confirmed to the President's office that they had been keeping an eye on William Patrick since 1939, but, "There has been no allegation of activities inimical to the interests of this country on their part."

What Hoover did not tell the President was that the FBI had taken no action against William Patrick because the British had told him that "he was one of us" a reference to the fact that under the code name of 'Pearl' he had been helping the British in Germany during the 1930s.

During the question and answer sessions that followed his US talks, William Patrick was constantly

13

William Patrick in London, aged 18.

being asked why he hadn't volunteered for service. His reply was always that he had tried to join the US forces but that he was being refused permission because of his name. He had had to fill in an Alien Personal History and Statement for the Queens County Local Alien's Board and they were sceptical about hiring a Hitler.

It would appear that another reason for his rejection into the armed forces was his honesty. Section 32 of this form asked him if he had any living relatives who were in, or had been in, the armed forces of the countries named. He said that he had two uncles who fell into this category: Thomas J Dowling who had served in the Royal Air Force from 1923 to 1926 and Adolf Hitler who had served as a corporal in the German army from 1914 to 1918. This did not go down well. He was rejected for the US Army in 1942 "because the Army does not like one of his relatives. He is the nephew of Adolf Hitler," said a news report at the time. William Patrick was disappointed but not surprised. "My name does make things a bit difficult."

However, he persevered in trying to join up and on 3 March 1942 wrote a three-page rambling, flowery letter to President Franklin D Roosevelt pleading for him to use his Presidential prerogative and give him permission. William Patrick told the President that he was: ... *the nephew and only descendant of the ill-famed Chancellor and Leader of Germany who today so despotically seeks to enslave the free and Christian peoples of the globe. All my relatives and friends soon will be marching for freedom and decency under the Stars and Stripes. For this reason, Mr President, I am respectfully submitting this petition to you to enquire as to whether I am allowed to join them in their struggle against tyranny and oppression?*

15

Eleven days later, Roosevelt's private secretary, General Edwin M Watson passed the letter on to the head of the FBI, J Edgar Hoover, and asked him to comment. In turn, on 20 March, Hoover asked his Assistant Director, PE Foxworth to investigate and for William Patrick Hitler to be "discreetly, thoroughly interviewed for pertinent data" to "determine his activities and loyalties."

The senior FBI agent assigned to the task, a TB White, interviewed a number of William Patrick's acquaintances, some of whom wished to remain anonymous. In her memoirs, Bridget says she too was interviewed by American authorities and Foxworth confirms this in a teletype message to Hoover. On 3 April 1942, White delivered his report saying that there was no indication that William Patrick was 'engaged in subversive activities'. And that he had no credit record.

One of those White interviewed was the anonymous Confidential Informant #2, an author whom William Patrick had asked to help him write about his experiences in Germany. White's report says: ... *informant #2 was to participate in writing the book as a ghost-writer, while the book was to bear William Patrick Hitler's name as the author. In preparation of the writing of this book Confidential Informant #2 informed that it was necessary for him to obtain from subject Hitler his entire life history and also all information concerning his contacts and relationships with Adolf Hitler.*

Informant #2 thought that William Patrick – described in the FBI report as being 6 feet 1 inch tall, 280 lbs, with dark brown hair and blue eyes – was extremely lazy with no initiative. He also said that William Patrick was extremely religious, which was probably due to the influence of his mother. This un-named author talked to William Patrick about the autobiography constantly for

WILLIAM PATRICK
HITLER

Nephew of Reichsfuhrer
ADOLPH HITLER

●

REVEALS THE SENSATIONAL
TRUTH ABOUT THE LEADERS
OF NAZI GERMANY TODAY

HEAR
HIS DARING
EXPOSÉ
OF INTRIGUE
AMONG THE
ENSLAVERS
OF EUROPE

wbf

41

Publicity poster advertising a lecture by William Patrick.

WILLIAM PATRICK HITLER

BORN IN ENGLAND to Hitler's half-brother Alois and an Irish mother, he was educated in English schools and did not meet his celebrated uncle until 1929 at the Nuremberg Congress of the Nazi Party. In 1933 William Patrick Hitler went to live in Germany and during the next six years was under the constant surveillance of Hitler himself and such dignitaries as Rudolf Hess and Ernst Wilhelm Bohle, in charge of all Germans living abroad and director of Fifth Column activities. Jailed during the "blood purge" of 1934, young Hitler was released through the intervention of British diplomatic officials.

He worked in the Opel automobile plant but was prevented from pursuing an engineering and sales career by a Fuhrer who felt his dignity insulted. Young Hitler was frequently called on the Chancellor's carpet and given unmistakable warning against revelation of Hitler family life, and his freedom to seek employment was curbed at every turn. A devout Catholic, he never subscribed to Nazi doctrines and observed with horror the attacks upon his Church. Finally, in 1939, he was told that he must accept German citizenship, but he slipped out of the Third Reich across to England where he met his mother and with her departed for America.

His story of the Nazi regime is unique, for he brings testimony of the true character of Hitler and his jealous rivals. Constantly threatened with Gestapo reprisal for his indiscretion, William Patrick Hitler has chosen to tell the truth of Hitler's background, his strange assortment of actress and young men friends, the cabals which surround Der Führer, the reaction of the German people to the barbarism of the Nazi party machine.

COMMENTS

"Young Patrick Hitler was so much better than I dared hope. . . . We had the largest attendance we've ever had at a Saturday meeting at which he spoke. He received an ovation when he finished. . . ."
—*President,* WISCONSIN EDUCATION ASSOCIATION

". . . impressed with his fairness in discussing a subject which might easily have shown bias. He was frank and yet pleasing in conducting the Forum following the main address. Even the most critical professors gave him credit for his astuteness and perspicacity in answering the many questions. . . ."
—*Superintendent,* PUBLIC SCHOOLS OF MONROE COUNTY, PA.

"We had a very good crowd—some 1,500 people. He made a very dignified presentation and had a very excellent question period. On a day of such vacations weather we would have had half as large a crowd with anyone else."
—*Secretary,* COATESVILLE (PA.) Y.M.C.A.

"Almost with his opening remarks, William Patrick 'had' his audience of six hundred. He not only 'had' them but continued by popular request way beyond the regular adjournment time."
—*Executive Secretary,* BUFFALO (N. Y.) ADVERTISING CLUB

"His audience was deeply interested in what he had to say. We were all impressed by the number of questions addressed to him after his lecture and by the quiet convincing manner in which he answered them."
—HORACE BUSHNELL MEMORIAL HALL, Hartford, Conn.

LECTURES

MY UNCLE ADOLF

Who the Fuhrer really is, how the Fuhrer really lives, what the Fuhrer really says in private and in public.

THE MYSTERY OF RUDOLF HESS

What led this high-ranking Nazi to surrender himself to the English is explained by his former ward.

WHAT THE GERMAN PEOPLE ARE THINKING

How the Nazis have silenced opposition among the German people and how the people prepare their day of revenge.

William Patrick Hitler discusses all topics dealing with Nazi Germany based on his intimate knowledge of its leaders and peoples.

Exclusive Management
WILLIAM B. FEAKINS, Inc.

500 FIFTH AVENUE
NEW YORK

VISTA DEL AR
PASADE?

44

Promotional leaflet for William Patrick.

three or four months before saying he didn't want to write it and then signed a release for a Eugene Lyons to be the ghost-writer.

Lyons was a journalist and writer, who in his younger days had been a Communist sympathiser and lived in Russia as a reporter. He later became the biographer of President Herbert Hoover and for a time was an editor with *Reader's Digest*.

The FBI report says that at a cocktail party William Patrick had become very friendly with an actress called Dot May Goodisky, who later introduced him to Lyons who then worked for the American *Mercury Magazine*. Lyons, fascinated by the Hitler story, persuaded Informant #2 to sign the release. This Informant #2 duly did and heard nothing more. Was Lyons, therefore, an unknown ghost-writer who helped William Patrick and Bridget in the writing of her memoirs?

In September 1943, William Patrick was interviewed by a Harvard psychoanalyst Walter Langer on behalf of the Office of Strategic Services – the fore-runner of the CIA. Langer had been asked by the OSS to do a psychological analysis of Adolf Hitler and to do so he needed to talk to as many of those who knew him as possible. The interview was primarily about Adolf Hitler's family situation leading up to and during his rise to power and William Patrick was an obvious person to see. Bridget was also interviewed by Langer, but there is no record of Langer's thoughts on this.

The interview throws further light on Adolf's relationship with his niece Geli. In her memoirs, Bridget says that Geli did not commit suicide as the Germans claimed, but that Hitler killed his own niece in a fit of incestuous jealousy, because she had unwisely told him that she was pregnant by her Jewish music teacher, a fact later confirmed by Hans Franck 'the Butcher of Poland' in his memoirs.

Franck had also been asked by Hitler in 1930 to make a top secret investigation into William Patrick, after Hitler had received a 'disgusting blackmail threat' from his 'loathsome relative'. This was a result of William Patrick writing to Hitler saying that Hitler's grandfather may have been an Austrian Jew.

The FBI report does not give any clues as to their recommendations to the President concerning William Patrick but, on 6 March 1944, the 33-year-old man – and still a British citizen – walked into the Local Draft Board in Long Island City and was inducted into the United States Navy. Mr Hitler was sent with other Navy recruits to the Navy Recruiting Station at 88 Vanderbilt Avenue to be assigned to a Louisiana boot camp. The following month, on 12 May, he formally joined up and was sworn in for active service with the US Navy at Algiers, Louisiana. His recruiting officer was one Gale K Hess, who is said to have welcomed William Patrick in front of press photographers with the phrase: "Glad to see you, Hitler, my name's Hess," presumably ignorant of the fact that Adolf Hitler had once asked Rudolph Hess, then his private secretary, to keep an eye on William Patrick when they met many years before.

The 112-page FBI investigation into William Patrick ends with the statement: 'In view of the fact that the subject is presently a member of the Armed Forces of the United States, no further investigation is being conducted.'

At the end of the war, having served his time in the US Navy's Medical Corps, William Patrick was honourably discharged – again the Americans using a

Seaman First Class William Patrick's,
official discharge from the US Navy

photo opportunity with his discharge officer Commander
Fey. As a serving member of the US forces, he would have
received an American Campaign Medal and the Second
World War Victory Medal. When asked what was the first
thing he was going to do after discharge, he replied, "See
my mother." Soon after, in January 1946, the office of
Naval Intelligence in Boston conducted an investigation
following William Patrick's request for naturalisation.

Bridget Hitler also played her part in the war effort at
the same time as her son. On 25 June 1941 she started
work at the headquarters of the British War Relief Society
at 730 Fifth Avenue (opposite Tiffany's). She told the *New
York Times* in a rich Irish brogue that it was, "a bit
ridiculous, but my name is Hitler and I'll work just as
hard as anybody, notwithstanding," when she walked in
to offer her services. Then she hastily explained that she

hoped to obtain an annulment of her marriage whilst in the country and "would dearly love" to become an American citizen but could not at that time because she was only there on a visitor's visa. "Hanging," Mrs Hitler declared, "would be too good for my brother-in-law."

Clearly Bridget and William Patrick had remained extremely close. They had moved from Liverpool to London together; worked for the same London engineering company; were fired at the same time for having Hitler as their surname and, as Bridget says in her memoirs, searched for new work together. When William Patrick, leaving his mother in London, went to look for work in Germany she cried; and, of course, they emigrated to New York together, sharing the same home during the war and living next door to each other in peace time.

In 1947, William Patrick married his German girl-friend, Phyllis Jean-Jacques, and they remained together until his death in 1987. They had met and dated in Germany during the 1930s, after being introduced by her brother; and they had kept in touch during the war through her sister.

As a civilian, William Patrick soon found work in the urology department of a New York hospital, before setting up his own business analysing blood samples for hospitals. He then made the decision to go into total obscurity, changing his name and settling in a small town. In choosing his new identity, William Patrick showed some considerable contradiction. Bizarrely, having spent most of the past few years criticising Hitler, for his new family name he chose Stuart-Houston – a corruption of Houston Stewart Chamberlain, the British born extreme anti-Semitic author, from whose book *The*

Foundations of the 19th Century, published in 1899, the Nazis had gleaned many of their racial ideologies. Chamberlain became a German citizen and married Richard Wagner's daughter Eva. Wagner was Adolf Hitler's favourite composer.

When William Patrick and Phyllis married, the couple moved to Silver Street, Patchogue, Long Island, a working class bay town near New York. Bridget moved with them, living next door at 67, and was quickly joined by her brother Thomas Dowling.

From their two-storey clapboard house in Silver Street, William Patrick and Phyllis raised four sons and from there he also ran his diagnostic blood lab. To their neighbours, they seemed like any other all-American family, despite some claiming they spoke German at home and with Phyllis often playing German music.

"They were just these four wild kids running around that little house" neighbour Teresa Ryther told the *New York Times*. "They were like any other kids on the block … American kids. It was almost as if they were rebelling against their German background and being intensely American. Inside the house it was very German, very European and the parents spoke German." They all graduated from Patchogue High School where their extrovert third son, Howard, was a cheer-leader.

The eldest son, Alexander Adolf, was born in 1949. It is interesting that despite William Patrick's public denunciations of his half brother, he chose to give his first born the German dictator's name. So it could be argued that there is an Adolf Hitler alive today.

"My father was a good guy," says Alex. "He came to the United States, he served in the US Navy. He had four kids and he had a pretty good life. My father was definitely anti-Nazi and anti-Hitler. I don't know why he called me Adolf. I wasn't there when he decided."

Alex is a very private man who kept his occupation so secret that neighbours at first thought he must be in the CIA. In fact he first worked in Macy's department store and then became a social worker counselling Vietnam veterans. Like two of his other brothers, Alex initially denied that there had been a pact between the brothers to ensure that the Hitler line did not continue, but eventually admitted: "Maybe my two brothers did, but I never did."

Louis, born in 1951, is the second son and together with Brian, the fourth son, runs a Long Island landscaping business. Like the three remaining brothers, he has never married and, like the other brothers is a registered Republican voter.

Howard Ronald, unlike the other brothers, did marry, although he never had children. In many ways he was the more out-going of the four, carving out a career away from Long Island and being the only one to work in Manhattan.

He joined the Inland Revenue as a service Special Agent, and was tragically killed in 1989 aged 32, when he was involved in a head-on crash with a car full of teenagers, which had veered across the road and smashed into him. He was on his way to serve a summons for money laundering. According to official records, he was the first Inland Revenue Service Special Agent to die in the line of duty. He had been married for about four years and had been a Special Agent for nearly 18 months.

Brian William, the youngest, was born in 1965 and is also single, having joined the pact never to have children so that the line would die out with them. He, like the other unmarried brothers, has been involved in serious relationships. For two of the brothers, at least two relationships quickly collapsed when the women they hoped to marry were told they would effectively become a Mrs Hitler and they were not prepared to face the consequences. One of the women was said to be Jewish, the other a Puerto Rican. Many of the then residents in the town of Patchogue had either served in the Second World War or had relatives who had died in Europe; consequently they would have been extremely sensitive to having Hitlers living among them.

William Patrick was as close to his sons and his wife as he was to his mother. "They were everything to him," said a neighbour.

Bridget Hitler died in 1969 and, even after her death, the family kept up the subterfuge, putting Hiller on the death certificate as her married name rather than Hitler. One of his sons recalled that the first time he had ever seen his father cry was after Brigid's death, writes David Gardner in his book *The Last of the Hitlers*.

By 1979, according to historian John Toland, when William Patrick was 67, he refused to discuss his past and wished to have absolutely nothing to do with his late uncle.

William Patrick died suddenly in November 1987, taking everyone by surprise. Apparently he developed a fever and was being treated for bronchial infection when he died in hospital only days later aged 76. Phyllis and her sons apparently considered burying him without a headstone, but in the end they decided to have a headstone and he was buried with Bridget.

Not long before she too died, in 2004, Phyllis said, "We were married a long time and my husband never wanted anyone to know who he was. Now my sons don't want anything to do with it. It was all a long time ago.

William Patrick shortly before his death in 1987.

There has been enough trouble with this name."

The family moved out of Silver Street in the mid-1990s when their house was sub-divided into a crowded boarding house for day labourers. It was sold again in 1999 and, in the subsequent renovations, German newspapers were found behind the wallboard.

Although William Patrick and Phyllis' four sons bear the surname of their parents, they are the last of the Hitler blood-line.

My Brother-in-law Adolf begins by describing in detail how a naive 17-year-old Bridget Dowling met and fell in love with the dashing 27-year-old Alois Hitler at the Dublin Horse Show in 1909. Although her family disapproved of her choice – with her father threatening to have Alois charged with kidnap – they eventually relented and the couple married in London. Bridget much later recalled that: *My father, rest his soul, was a real Irishman, he was a farm labourer from Kilnamanagh. He would not hear tell of a wedding to a foreigner. Alois and I used to meet every afternoon in the museum and make plans to elope. Four months later, when Alois had saved enough money, we went to England on the night boat and came to London. I wrote to my mother and said I would not return until we got permission to marry. She talked my father around and he gave his consent and we were married on June 3 1910, at Marylebone Register Office.*

On 12 March 1911 – nine months and nine days after their London wedding – their only child, William Patrick, was born in the couple's pleasant flat at 102 Upper Stanhope Street in the Toxteth district of Liverpool. Bridget's stern father William had made sufficient peace with the couple for him to come to Liverpool for William Patrick's baptism. Bridget tells how she and Alois immediately had their constant differences of opinion, this time on what to call the child. Alois favoured 'Willie', while Bridget insisted on 'Pat'.

Life in the Hitler family was hardly idyllic, according to Mrs Hitler – or Cece as Alois called her. Alois had a

Alois Hitler.

'volatile, bohemian nature' and was an irresponsible, chronic gambler who was 'always about to make his fortune'. He changed jobs four times during their first two years of marriage, quickly moving from London, after their marriage, to Liverpool, where he opened a small restaurant in Dale Street. Liverpool at that time had a large German community, so Alois would have been very much at home. He soon sold the restaurant and bought a small boarding house in Parliament Street. He then traded in that business for a hotel in Mount Pleasant and eventually went bankrupt. Undeterred by this failure, he plunged into the safety razor business, which Mrs Hitler describes as 'a novelty at the time'.

There were times, says Bridget, when she didn't have enough money to buy milk for their baby. But there were also times when Alois managed to make a lot of money gambling. One incident she describes has Alois coming home, throwing a wad of money on the table and declaring, "We are rich!" He told her that he had won the money on the Grand National at Aintree. He swept Bridget into his arms and within a couple of hours had carried her off for a whirlwind tour of the gambling tables of Le Touquet in France.

When Alois hit it big with his gambling he was generous and often sent money to his sisters in Vienna – his full sister Angela (Adolf's half-sister) and his half sister Paula (Adolf's full sister).

It was after a big win at the gambling tables in 1912 that Alois began dreaming of building his safety-razor salesman's business into an international sales organisation, with Angela's husband, Anton Raubal at the head of the Central European division. He sent some travel money for Angela and Anton to come to Liverpool from Vienna to discuss the project more fully. Bridget says, *We went to Lime Street station. Instead of Anton and Angela, a shabby young man approached and offered Alois his hand. It was my husband's younger brother, Adolf who came in his place.*

Alois was furious. He and Adolf did not get on and he was the last person he wanted to see. "He's just a good for nothing," Alois told Bridget. Bridget says of Adolf: *He remained in his room and slept in bed most of the time. A less interesting and pre-possessing house guest I cannot imagine. His colour was so bad, his eyes looked peculiar, I felt sorry for him. He had no luggage, one frayed shirt – so worn, it wasn't worth turning. Thinking back, I found him only weak and spineless. He did nothing but play with the baby in the kitchen.*

At that time, writes historian Ian Kershaw, Adolf, 'lived a life of parasitic idleness – funded, provided for, looked after and cosseted by a doting mother.' Not too far a picture from how he expected Bridget to treat him.

Even a decade later Joseph Goebbels agreed with Bridget's view of young Adolf. In the 1920s he wrote in a newspaper he then edited: *The Führer does not change. He is the same now as he was when he was a boy. If we glance at his boyhood we find that Hitler was far from a model student. He studied what he wanted to study and did fairly well in these subjects. Things which did not interest him he simply ignored, even though his marks were 'unsatisfactory' or 'failing'. For over a year before his mother died, in 1908, he did nothing, as far as can be determined, except lie around the house, or occasionally paint a few water-colours. Although they were in difficult financial circumstances he did not seek work or try to improve himself in school. He was self-willed, shy and inactive.*

According to the memoirs, he also spent time sight-seeing around Liverpool being very impressed with the amount of merchant navy there was passing through the

A copy of William Patrick's birth certificate.

Upper Stanhope Street, c1935. Number 102 (demolished during the War) is marked with an arrow.

port. In his book on the British Security Co-ordination – a wartime body linking secret services in the US and Britain – spy-master William Stephenson confirms this: *BSC records suggest that Adolf Hitler spent much of his time watching the flow of sea traffic through Liverpool to the four corners of the British Empire.* The memoirs also say that Adolf went to London with Alois, where he managed to talk his way into the machinery room at Tower Bridge and, according to his American family, he even paid a visit to Ireland.

Tensions were high between the three of them and early on in Adolf's visit Alois failed to persuade him to emigrate to America, even offering to pay his fare. Eventually, Adolf did decide to leave. Alois, happy with this, gave him the money to buy his return train ticket, advising him to go to Munich. He left in February, 1913, but may not have gone straight to Germany, as in April that year he was in Vienna to claim an inheritance due on his birthday on the 24th of that month. With that money, he then travelled on to Munich.

A year later, in May 1914, Alois left his wife and three-year-old son in Liverpool for Germany, saying he was going to launch an English razor company in Europe, but Bridget suspected he was going to play roulette. However, the First World War erupted the same week Alois planned to return home to be reunited with his family and consequently he was stuck in Europe.

According to the son, Bridget – a staunch Catholic and "a rigid person" – had left Alois three or four times in the early years of their marriage because he had threatened to hit her baby.

William Patrick was just 20 months old when Adolf turned up in Liverpool and just three when his father left home. He had as normal an upbringing as he could in the circumstances. He was first educated at St Margaret's Church of England School in Toxteth, Liverpool – despite his mother being a Catholic.

In 1973 Albert Whitehead, a retired electricity installation inspector, told the *Liverpool Daily Post*: *I first got to know Willie in the early 1920s when we both went to St Margaret's Church of England School, Princes Road, Princes Park. He lived in the same street as I did. We became friends and he joined our scout troop, the 222nd Liverpool, which later became the 11th Toxteth.*

He was in my patrol, in the Curlews, of which I was the leader. Willie and his mother eventually left the neighbourhood to live in London. I know Willie went to Germany to meet Uncle Adolf, and I can remember the Pathé News showing Willie Hitler sailing to America.

Willie was a quiet, pale boy. He was a Roman Catholic, although he went to our school, and he often went to the Anglican Cathedral with me.

The Hitler family's former home in Upper Stanhope Street was not hit by a bomb, as is widely believed, but it was badly damaged by a bomb that fell in the street and which destroyed my own former home at 115. Of our houses, 113, 115, 117 and 119 were destroyed by a stick of bombs but no one was killed. I believe it was the last stick of bombs to fall on Liverpool.

Arthur Bryan of Crosby, near Liverpool, was also at school with William Patrick. He remembered being in Dieppe at the beginning of the Second World War: 'I ran into an old school-mate,' he recalled in the *Post*, 'and he said to me, "Remember Willie Hitler?" That's when I realised that Willie had always talked about this uncle of his who, he said, was a General in Germany.'

Short of money, Bridget first worked in the box-office

of the Olympian Theatre in Liverpool, while taking singing lessons to fulfil a childhood dream of going on the stage. She joined a number of theatre groups before touring with Harry Lauder's company. On one tour through Europe her company ended up in Monte Carlo. To her surprise, while performing as a chorus girl in a show, she saw her husband, whom she had earlier been told by a friend of his, had died in the Ukraine. Alois was with 'a woman of rather a Mongolian cast of features, with slanty eyes and dark hair.' Alois, seeing Bridget, whispered in his friend's ear and the couple hurriedly left.

Because of her burgeoning stage career, Bridget and her son moved to London and William Patrick went to Ashford College, a boarding school in Middlesex where he studied accountancy. On one of her visits to see him she was surprised when William Patrick showed her a pile of newspaper cuttings telling of an unsuccessful coup d'état in Munich. "Adolf Hitler," he said to his mother. "He must be my uncle."

William Patrick, wanting to know if this man actually was his uncle, wrote to the Mayor of Munich asking if he could get in touch with Adolf Hitler. To his surprise he received a 'cold' reply from Alois, who was in Hamburg.

On receipt of William Patrick's letter, an officious Munich civil servant started his own investigation into Alois and found that he had married again – to Hedwig Heidemann, with whom he had had a son. Alois was charged with bigamy. However, he was spared jail when Bridget agreed to intervene on his behalf. According to both Bridget's memoirs and the OSS report, Alois wrote to Bridget 'begging her to have mercy on him and that if she did not press the suit he would send her money for their support regularly and threatened to commit suicide if she did press suit.' She agreed not to proceed if he sent them money monthly; as a result of Bridget's consent, the court found Alois guilty but gave him a one-year suspended prison sentence. He never sent any money.

After leaving school at 17, William Patrick started working for Benhan & Son Ltd, an engineering company in Wigmore Street, London. Some time later his mother joined him there. They worked for the firm until 1932 when they were sacked for bearing the Hitler surname.

In 1928, the year after he started work, William Patrick paid his first visit to Germany when he went on a two-week holiday to visit his father in Berlin. He returned the following year when he and his father went to the National Socialist Party Congress in Nuremberg where they stayed for about five days. It was here that William Patrick saw Adolf Hitler – he was addressing a crowd of 30,000 said William Patrick in a letter to his mother. But they didn't meet up. 'We were hoping to get a chance to talk to him,' he said in the letter, 'but Father … said it was impossible, as Uncle Adolf didn't want to mix his family with business.'

Back in Germany for the third year running, William Patrick describes in another letter to his mother how he met Uncle Adolf for the first time since he came to fame.

We had just finished dinner last night, and Father was unfolding the evening paper, when the door bell rang. It was Uncle Adolf, wearing a trench coat with the collar turned up and a homburg hat pulled down in the front. Underneath he was wearing an ordinary blue business suit. He looks much better than in uniform.

Alois was surprised and asked Adolf why he had come. "I wanted to meet this Englishman," he said with 'a twinkle in his eye'.

Uncle Adolf had been looking at me from time to time as though he was curious about me. Now he turned to me and said: "And you, you English boy, what is your opinion on the Jewish question? What are they doing about it in England?" I was really embarrassed but tried to tell him as well as I could in broken German that we didn't have a Jewish problem in England. "In Germany, it would be different," he shouted at me.

It would appear that as soon as William Patrick was old enough to realise the value of his relationship to his uncle, he was actively encouraged by his mother to capitalise on it. Indeed, Bridget, in the memoirs, substantiates this impression. She is at all times naively anxious to present herself as the good mother, the pretty deserted wife, the innocent bystander – but someone who needed money.

'Mrs Hitler chafed more and more under her poverty,' writes Langer, in his OSS report on Hitler. She decided again to try and get some form of support, as she was tired of Alois' broken promises, so she started to negotiate a deal with the American Hearst newspaper group. She wrote to Alois asking for more details about Adolf's younger days but was surprised when a reply came back from Adolf. She and William Patrick were given tickets to go to Munich for a conference 'where they found Adolf in a perfect rage. He summoned a family counsel at which Adolf, Angela, Alois, William Patrick and his mother were present,' says Langer's report. The report continues: *The gist of what Adolf said was now that he was getting some importance, the family need not think that they could climb on his back and get a free ride to fame. He claimed that any release to Hearst newspapers involving his family would destroy his chances of success, in view of Alois' record. It was finally suggested that William Patrick and his* *mother return to London … and say that Adolf Hitler was not the uncle they had supposed … and was no kin to them. Hitler was pleased with this solution. He handed Alois $2000 to cover their expenses while in Munich … and to give Mrs Hitler what was left over when these expenses were paid. Alois … did everything except pass over what was left of the sum and promised to send it through the mail which would be much safer, but it never arrived.*

It is not surprising, therefore, that Adolf Hitler was less than delighted at the constant arrival in Germany of his Liverpool nephew. Then, as now, scandal could mean the end of a political career and as a result of this caution, Hitler was fanatically secretive about his background and, says the FBI report: *At the termination of this interview, subject advised that the Führer then introduced him to Rudolf Hess and advised Hess that William Patrick Hitler was under his supervision and that he was to find him a suitable position.*

William Patrick's attitude to Adolf is ambivalent. There is evidence that during visits to Germany in the 1930s he was treated with scorn by Hitler and his subordinates; yet he was still able to tell the *London Daily Express* on 22 November 1937: I*n Germany I am a private individual and in England I am a private individual. I have no authority to make any political statements and I would not want to say anything to embarrass my uncle. My mother is Irish and a good Catholic and I find it very difficult to convert her to National Socialism. There are many things she feels very bitter about.*

When interviewed during the Second World War by the FBI, William Patrick told them that Adolf Hitler had given him 500 Marks in 1933 and – says the report – put him under the supervision of Rudolph Hess.

In 1934 William Patrick was arrested in Germany, following the attempted plot to overthrow Hitler by

Captain Ernst Rohm – an event which Bridget describes in detail in her memoirs.

The FBI investigation also said that as well as the attempt to get money out of Hitler by threatening to publish the fact that he had Jewish blood in him, William Patrick had also tried another … *mild form of blackmail against Adolf Hitler in order to secure for himself a job of importance with little work attached to the position. His threat was that he, 'subject Hitler' (ie William Patrick) had intimated to him (Confidential Informant #2) that this threat was to the effect that he, subject Hitler, might reveal that his father Alois Hitler had deserted his wife Brigid* (sic) *Elizabeth Dowling Hitler and had left her to shift for herself; further, that in the meantime, Alois Hitler had married again without obtaining a divorce from Brigid Hitler. Confidential Informant #2 stated that this blackmail had succeeded in a mild way, in view of the fact that subject Hitler was given a few minor jobs as a bookkeeper. However, he did eventually secure a position with the Opel Automobile Works, which is a subsidiary of the General Motors Corporation.*

Patrick initially went to work on the assembly line, but Adolf Hitler would not give him permission to send some of his wages back to his mother in England. He was soon transferred to sales. However, the Gestapo were told, and they informed Adolf that William Patrick was using the Hitler name to sell cars. William Patrick was 'advised by the Gestapo to discontinue these practices.' Over and over again Hitler had warned him about trying to cash in on their relationship.

In the FBI report, Informant #2 says that William Patrick told him that he wanted a better job than Adolf was prepared to give him and because Hitler didn't do this, William Patrick was opposed to him. William Patrick confirmed this to an audience at the 101 Club in New York, saying the real reason he left Germany was the fact that his uncle would not obtain a position for him and not, as he had also said, because of Hitler's persecution of the Catholic Church. But then he tended to give slightly different responses to different audiences.

Apart from annoyance at Adolf's lack of interest in her son, Bridget was also bitter about her nationality. On her marriage to Alois she had become an Austrian citizen, and when Austria was annexed by Germany she became a German. This caused her no problems until the late 1930s when relations between Germany and Britain became strained. Then she suddenly realised how much she wanted to become British. In the same 1937 interview in the *Daily Express* William Patrick was quoted as saying, "Recently the Austrian consulate refused to renew her papers, so that now she has no country."

A year later they were living in a small semi-detached housed in Hornsey, in north London, and Bridget was still trying, without success, to become a British subject. She is quoted, again in the *Daily Express*, as follows: *I want to get back my British nationality. I've seen the Home Office and they want to help me, but unless my marriage can be dissolved I must remain an alien. Just to think that I, Bridget Dowling that was, am now a German subject since Hitler took Austria. As a Catholic I don't believe in divorce. My husband and I are separated, but that isn't good enough for the Home Office. Nowadays it's a bit embarrassing to be Mrs Hitler, but the people who know me don't mind, and the others don't matter. At heart, I'm still Bridget Dowling, but ho! It's my British nationality I want.*

In this period Bridget twice wrote to the German Embassy in London, attempting to persuade them to pay her some money on which to live. In June 1938 she also wrote to Otto Karlowa the leader of the Nazi party in London, asking him to supply her 'with the means to take a large house.' She wrote that her poor financial position was a 'poor reward for the part I have played.' In September 1938, Karlowa seems to have obtained permission from Germany for the payment to Mrs Hitler of a regular allowance, but it is doubtful if this allowance was ever paid.

During this time, William Patrick also wrote to Ernst 'Putzi' Hanfstaengl, the half-American Foreign Press Chief of the Nazi Party and provides 'the only evidence we have regarding William Patrick's political sympathies' states the FBI report. This evidence was in a letter Hanfstaengl received from William Patrick at the end of January 1938. In this letter to Hanfstaengl, who was then living in London, William Patrick refers to a report that he might be writing a book about 'my uncle and Germany in an adverse manner'. He says that the report is quite untrue: *The very keen regard which I cherish for the German people, as well as the respect I have for the Führer, would probably prohibit my acting detrimentally to either of them. In view of the fact that I have never done anything to bring discredit upon my uncle, or my name, but have had always the earnest desire to prove my loyalty to him, in spite of the hardships I may have suffered, I feel your original advice to me to stick at all costs to my name, even if I did constitute a problem by doing so, is very sound.* He returned to Germany soon after.

A year later, in early January 1939, Bridget had moved to 27 Priory Gardens, Highgate, north London, and had begun to take in lodgers. In fact, on 20 January 1939, Bridget Hitler appeared at Highgate Police Court, where she had been summonsed for failing to pay £9 13s 10d due in rates. After the hearing, at which she was given six weeks to pay, she said, referring to the Karlowa promise, "I was expecting some money from Germany, but I can't say anything about it."

In February, William Patrick was 'smuggled out of Germany' with the help of a British intelligence agent called Fenton and a magician called Bunny Aulden. William Patrick later told the FBI that the reasons he left were because of the persecution of the Catholic Church; the fact that Adolf Hitler wouldn't give him a sinecure job – a job in which he was well paid and had little to do; because he never subscribed to Nazi doctrines and because Adolf wanted him to become a German citizen.

It could also be that, with the onset of war, William Patrick had to flee because he was about to be exposed as a British agent. British intelligence told the FBI in 1942 that 'he was one of us', working for the British in Germany under the alias of 'Pearl'. And it would appear from Bridget's memoirs that his handler was the British agent Fenton, whom Bridget had visited in London.

Back in London, William Patrick was approached by a literary agent to lecture in the United States, so mother and son decided to emigrate.

Bridget's husband's activities are also fairly well documented. Alois Hitler was a waiter, a gambler, an extrovert, a traveller and a fantasist who was always going to make money from the current fad, such as safety razor blades. He was twice jailed for theft – in 1900 for five months when he was an apprentice waiter, followed by an eight-month stretch in 1902. He was also, of course, a bigamist, having been found guilty in Hamburg in March 1924 for marrying Hedwig Heidemann.

They had a son, Heinz Hitler, who unlike his half-brother was a Nazi. Heinz attended an élite Nazi military academy and was aspiring to be an officer, then he joined the Wehrmacht as a signals NCO with the 23rd Potsdamer Artillery Regiment in 1941, and he took part in Operation Barbarossa, the invasion of the Soviet Union. On 10 January 1942 he was captured by Soviet forces and sent to a Moscow military prison, where he died, aged 21, after several months of interrogation and torture.

Alois moved to Dublin in 1909 and got a job as a waiter in the Shelbourne Hotel. But on his days off the fantasist in him took over and he posed as a wealthy hotelier on a European tour studying the industry.

His suit and hat were of the latest fashion, wrote Bridget. *A heavy gold-watch chain stretched across his cream-coloured waistcoat. He wore two rings on his little left finger, one a diamond and the other a ruby. In addition he wore a pearl tie-pin. His moustache was of the handlebar variety – waxed and turned up at the ends. To my interested eyes he represented the height of elegance.*

During most of the 1930s Alois kept a small inn in a Berlin suburb, but in 1937 he branched out in a big way by opening new café-restaurants in Berlin's fashionable West End, first in Wittensburgplatz and then, during the war, in the Kurfurstendamn. In this restaurant he played a canny game of appearing on the one hand to keep out of politics, while at the same time trading on his brother's name, even flying the swastika over the entrance. The personal animosity that once existed between the two seems by now to have gone, because, in a 1938 will, Adolf left Alois 60,000 Marks. The will was not discovered until 1953, when Alois was in Hamburg. It is not known if he received any money.

Although he managed to keep his restaurant open

throughout the war, Alois became something of an embarrassment to the German authorities. In 1945 he tried to slip through the occupation forces by changing his name to Eberle, but he was arrested for being in possession of false identification papers and was handed over to the British. A few weeks later, in August, he was released. A statement by the military authorities ran: *It is clear to us that he has led a perfectly blameless existence, being absolutely scared stiff of being associated in any way with the former Führer's activities.*

Soon after, and now suffering from rheumatism, he and Hedwig, his common-law wife, moved to Hamburg, where they lived with friends while waiting in vain to return to the American sector of Berlin to reclaim his restaurant. He had now legally changed his name from Hitler – not to Eberle, but to Hiller – because, "I had never found the name Hitler any help and it is now a positive disadvantage."

Eventually, in the early 1950s, he took up politics for the first time, being associated with an extreme right-wing nationalistic movement, of which, according to reports, he soon became leader. This political party seems to have foundered before it really got started, and by 1953 he was known to have been seen selling portraits of his brother Adolf to tourists, having signed them himself as Alois Hitler. He was quoted in that year as saying: "Adolf seemed ashamed of having a brother running a wine shop." He died in Hamburg on 20 May 1956, aged 74.

THE MEMOIRS

Bridget's memoirs make remarkable reading. She claims that from November 1912 to April 1913, Adolf Hitler was an unwelcome guest in the flat at 102 Upper Stanhope Street, Liverpool; that Hitler, in a fit of incestuous passion, killed his own niece, Geli; and that as a young man he had been a draft-dodger who had lived on charity in an old people's home rather than find work or serve in the army.

Bridget wrote the memoirs in America during and after the Second World War and the unevenness of style suggests that she must have had some sort of professional guidance, as well as the undoubted help of her son William Patrick Hitler. The typewritten document, entitled *My Brother-in-Law Adolf*, is 220 pages long. It is undated and unfinished – ending on a comma halfway through a sentence and with William Patrick leaving Germany with the help of Bunny Aulden and just before mother and son emigrated to America. There is no handwriting on the document, save the occasional word crossed out and another penned above it.

The manuscript came into the hands of the New York Public Library in 1959, or 1960, as part of a collection of papers belonging to the late Dr Edmund Pauker who died in 1962. Pauker was a European-born theatrical agent, a play-broker and literary agent for playwrights, particularly Hungarian and German playwrights, the most notable of whom was Ferenc Molnar. How Pauker came into possession of the memoirs is not known. His son John stated: *My father, like any theatrical agent, received literally thousands of manuscripts. I don't have the faintest idea how he came by that one, and I don't recall seeing it when I went through his papers after his death. Believe me, I would have kept it myself if I had come across it.*

Why were the memoirs never published at the time? Well, they were clearly incomplete, and perhaps Pauker decided that the market was already glutted with recollections of Hitler; maybe he thought he was sitting on a gold mine and was merely waiting for Bridget to finish what she had begun; or then again, he might never have known he had them.

The reason why Bridget's manuscript ends so abruptly – and before her US life – is open to both conjecture and contradiction. Perhaps she did finish the document, as some of her grandchildren have suggested and the final pages were then lost. Alex, William Patrick's eldest son, also said that the memoir, which includes details of Hitler's English visit, was essentially factual and was written jointly by William Patrick and his mother. "My father also told me that Hitler had visited Ireland."

Or was it that Bridget and William Patrick – and a ghost-writer – simply lost interest? In any event, the library collated the available pages and thought them of sufficient importance to be bound in hard covers and preserved in the Manuscript Room, where rare books and manuscripts are kept behind grilled doors and where only researchers showing special passes issued by the library administration could gain access to manuscripts such as Bridget's. Furthermore, the library was convinced enough of its authenticity to enter the memoirs in its catalogue file – a doubtful fate for a fraudulent document.

The mere fact that the NY Public Library took the manuscript seriously would seem to disprove some eminent historians, including Hugh Trevor-Roper, who have dismissed the memoirs as 'a work of fiction without a grain of truth'. This is clearly wrong, based on the evidence that has now come to light, and even at the time was written with an emotional reaction rather than an objective one. The sheer banality of the writing would indicate that not only did Bridget write them, but that the memoirs are true. She describes Adolf as lazy around her Toxteth home, sleeping a lot and that 'during his Liverpool stay Adolf hadn't picked up enough English to ask directions to the station.' This laziness is acknowledged by the eminent Hitler historian Ian Kershaw who writes, 'He had grown into an idle, resentful, rebellious, sullen, stubborn, and purposeless teenager.'

Some historians say that there are too many discrepancies in what is written about Adolf in Liverpool, to take the memoirs seriously. However, extensive research at the time, and since, has shown there to be few, if any, such inaccuracies.

It has always been well known that there was a lost year in Adolf's life. Hitler never mentioned this year and it wasn't in any of his writings. His failure to be accepted into the Viennese art school, his living rough in doss houses and the fact that he fled in order to avoid being called up in the Austrian army – a draft dodger – meant that he wished to keep this part of his life secret while plotting his rise in German politics.

According to Kershaw, while there are no records of Hitler's movements between countries, 'There is actually an eye witness to Adolf Hitler's presence in the men's home in Vienna in February 1913, at a time when he is supposed to be in Liverpool.' However, this witness has never been identified. It is known that the home kept scrupulous records of its residents and these records show that he did leave the home at the time the memoirs say he left Liverpool. It could also be that this witness was wrong by only a few days. It is known that Hitler was in Vienna at this time because on his 24th birthday, 20 April 1913, Hitler was due to inherit his share of his father's inheritance. And on 16 May a Linz court confirmed that he would receive a sizeable sum, and that this would be sent to him at his address in Vienna. This enabled him to go to Munich in order, he hoped, to study art – and the sorting out of an inheritance would be a very good reason to leave Liverpool.

The waters were muddied by both Beryl Bainbridge's *Young Adolf* – her very funny novel about Hitler which, of course, is pure fiction – and her subsequent interviews. Of her novel, the idea for which came from the *Daily Post* articles, Beryl wrote in 2001: *I wrote a fictional account, one wholly inspired by that first encounter at Lime Street station. Just imagine the scene – the belch of steam as the train drew in, and out of the swirling mist the emergence of Adolf, shabby, 23 years old, and yet to make his bloody boot-print on history.*

Beryl had Adolf working in the Adelphi hotel as a waiter, when in fact at that time the hotel had been demolished and was being rebuilt. Other stories reflect the wit of imaginative Liverpudlians, with one man actually claiming that Hitler lived next door to him and they used to go together to watch Everton at Goodison Park.

Even Kershaw admits, 'Hitler was frequently inaccurate or careless with detail …' and that, 'The historical record of Adolf's early years is very sparse. His own account in *Mein Kampf* is inaccurate in detail and coloured in interpretation.'

The remaining members of Hitler's family contradict themselves in relation to the memoirs. At different times, they say the memoirs are a fake; then they say this is actually how they finished – on a comma and incomplete – and then they say that Bridget actually finished her memoirs, but they do not want them published.

For example, William's wife, Phyllis, said that: "It was all made up" and Alex, their eldest son, said: "We read the book and it was the funniest thing I ever saw in my life." However, he later said that it was all true. Furthermore, he said the remaining manuscript was actually completed and the NY library only had the first half.

As well as Ian Kershaw, among those most critical of the suggestion that Hitler ever visited Liverpool is Robert Waite. As Waite rightly points out, Bridget would have been aware that the early biographies of Hitler spoke of a 'lost year' during the Vienna period in which virtually nothing was known about him. Therefore, says Waite, she would have felt safe in filling this gap by having Adolf go to England to visit her family for the entire period. Waite gives a number of reasons for believing that Bridget invented parts of her diary. Some are trivial – such as that she mistakes the colour of Geli's hair. Some are mere matters of opinion, or point of view – 'I found him weak and spineless'. 'Spineless he was not,' says Waite, but at that time, as a young man, it was well known that Hitler was extremely lazy and idle.

However, both Waite and Kershaw deduce two weighty arguments from the silence about his 'missing' year: firstly, the Viennese authorities imply that Hitler was in Vienna during the time that Bridget claims he was in Liverpool, while the British immigration authorities have no record of his entry, and secondly, Hitler never spoke of a trip to Liverpool to anyone.

Taking Waite's the first point, it should be noted that

it is just as easy to claim that Hitler was not in Vienna as it is to claim that he was, and the honest answer must be that we simply cannot independently prove the matter one way or the other – even though one man, Karl Honisch, did claim to have been in Vienna with Hitler some of the time. Since it was an offence to leave the country without express permission – not to mention the offences of avoiding conscription and travelling under a false name – Adolf is unlikely to have broadcast his intention to leave by using his own name and he could have used Honisch as a cover, in order to avoid even more trouble. As for alien regulations in Britain, before 1914 these did not exist. In 1905 an Act covered the control of steerage passengers, the infirm and the sick, other than this, regulation was extremely lax, and Home Office officials say that it could have been easily contravened. Home Office officials also comment that even if the authorities had kept some sort of records, it would be impossible to check them now.

Their second argument is perhaps slightly stronger. There is no mention of a visit to England in any of Hitler's speeches, books, or lengthy 'Table Talk'; nor is there mention of it in any authentic memoir written by others who knew him. Heinz LingeLange, his valet of ten years' service, says flatly, that with the exception of brief trips to Italy and Paris, the Führer had "visited no other country". Lloyd George, the Duke of Windsor, Unity Mitford and many other British personalities conducted long intimate conversations with Hitler about every topic under the sun, and there is no mention of him having discussed such a visit to any of them. It is arguable that he may have wished to keep the visit quiet, either because he was ashamed of it, or because he felt it might prejudice the myth of his resolute progress to power. And it is known that Hitler was fanatical about keeping his family life private. For example, there is no mention of Alois, William Patrick's father, in *Mein Kampf.*

On the other hand, it has to be admitted by the sceptics that, as a whole, Bridget's memoirs are not over-written and in many ways rely on facts so trivial they would be hard to make up. Apart from the few melodramatic touches here and there, she writes simply and sensibly, and her description of Hitler's arrival in Liverpool is circumstantial and convincing in itself.

The main doubt about the memoirs concerns Hitler's alleged murder of his niece, Geli Raubal. It is said that Hitler was briefly away from Munich when Geli died, and that he raced home to find her dead. If this is to be believed, he could not have shot Geli himself, as Bridget states. Nor could Leo, Geli's brother, have taken the revenge on Hitler she describes; Hitler would have had him removed. Far from removing him, when Leo was captured on the Russian front, Hitler intervened to have him exchanged. Moreover a different version by Bridget of the event is recorded in Ernst Hanfstaengl's book *The Missing Years.*

Walter Langer says in his report that Geli's brother Leo held Uncle Adolf responsible for Geli's death.

William Patrick, according to Langer's report, also met Geli several times and says that she was 'rather attractive in a peasant sort of way'. He says she was good-natured and rather pleasant company. 'When asked if she ever mentioned her uncle, she said that Hitler insisted that she accompany him wherever he went and it was very embarrassing for her.' William Patrick also says that Geli could speak a little English and that the only jewellery she wore was a golden swastika given to her by Hitler, whom she called Uncle Alf. In a letter to Bridget, William Patrick says: I guess that Geli is the only one Uncle Adolf is affectionate with. She told me even when he is in a savage mood … if she begins to cry he pulls himself out of it and comforts her … Only once did he lose his temper with her. That was one night when she was out late for a concert and a boy brought her home. Uncle Adolf was furious and forbade her to go out with boys at all. He wants to take absolute possession of her.

William Patrick said in 1939 that Hitler "is charged generally by many close to him of Geli's murder." She had been found dead on 19 September 1931, aged 23, at the Munich home she shared with Hitler, with his army revolver on the floor and an unfinished letter on the table. The death was said to have had a shattering effect on Hitler. Although it was said that Hitler was in Hamburg at the time, William Patrick said in a 1939 speech: *After she was discovered dead, Hitler ran sobbing out of his house and almost collapsed in the arms of Goering, who arranged all the burial details for the girl. They have a way of arranging these affairs in Nazi Germany.*

It is said by, among others, Alois' second wife, that Hitler became infuriated when Geli told him she was pregnant by her Jewish music teacher and tried to attack her with a riding whip before being stopped by his sister, Angela. Later that night Hitler and Geli were said to have been heard in a shouting match and the next morning she was found dead.

Bridget, in her memoirs, says that Hitler cried, "I am the murderer." Goering apparently then said, "Tell… the truth, that Geli committed suicide." He turned to Geli's mother. Angela and said: "My Führer was not even here."

And this alleged absence became the keynote of Adolf's alibi, ignoring the fact that even for Hitler it would have been impossible to get back from Hamburg in time for witnesses to have seen him at his flat.

Geli's death also occurred on a night when the entire Hitler household staff was off duty, except for a deaf worker, Frau Dachs.

The coroner's verdict was suicide, based on the fact that her door had been locked from the inside; no post-mortem was conducted, although a doctor estimated that her death had occurred the previous day, 18 September. However Geli was buried in hallowed ground by a Catholic priest, Father Johann Pant, who a few years later wrote to a French newspaper: 'From the fact I gave her a Catholic burial you can draw your own conclusions.'

Whether it was murder or suicide, Hitler sank into a profound depression, which lasted for several years, particularly during the Christmas holidays, when he wandered around Germany alone. During the first days after the funeral, Gregor Strasser remained with him in order to prevent him from committing suicide. At the time Strasser was the Reich Organisation Leader and had just reorganised the whole Nazi party structure, both in its regional formation and its management hierarchy. However, Strasser's star soon began to fall because it is believed that he had a brief affair with Geli and that Geli disclosed intimate details of Hitler's perversions and possible sexual impotence to him.

During the 1934 Nazi Party purge, known as 'The Night of the Long Knives', Strasser was imprisoned and then assassinated on Hitler's personal order by the Berlin Gestapo on 30 June 1934. The assassins shot through a window into Strasser's cell, eventually killing him.

Ernts Hanfstaengl, the Foreign Press Chief of the Nazi Party, writes in his book *Hitler – the Missing Years* that he was visited in London in the autumn of 1937 by Bridget Hitler. *She maintains that the immediate family knew well that the cause of Geli's suicide was the fact that she was pregnant by a young Jewish art teacher in Linz whom she had met in 1928 and wanted to marry at the time of her death.* Hanfstaengl also called her an ... *empty-headed little slut, with the coarse sort of bloom of a servant girl with no brains or character. She was perfectly content to preen herself in her fine clothes, and certainly never gave any impression of reciprocating Hitler's twisted tenderness.*

But this cynical view could have been as a result of Hitler's close friendship with Hanfstaengl's elder sister Erna.

Despite what Kershaw says, a lot of what Bridget wrote is historically accurate. As is clear from the memoirs, from his own writing, and from the interviews he gave over a period of time, William Patrick, encouraged by his mother, played on the uncle/nephew connection, hoping for considerable financial gain, particularly from his visits to Germany. The miserable sums of money he was given annoyed them both, and it is clear that Bridget tried to force Adolf's hand by selling their story to the American Hearst group. The memoirs state that she did this innocently at the request of Alois. When, in 1930, Adolf found out about an article William Patrick had written *My Uncle Adolf*, he flew into a rage, ordering William Patrick to visit him.

During the subsequent meeting, as the memoirs state, Adolf laid into William Patrick with a vengeance. Luckily for Bridget and her account, there was a witness to this. Hans Frank, later head of the General Government of

Poland and formerly Hitler's lawyer, who was subsequently hanged at Nuremberg, describes Hitler's anger. While waiting to be executed for his war crimes, Frank wrote his own memoirs, *Im Schatten des Galgens* (In the Shadow of the Gallows), in which he described the Führer's rage at his nephew's demands for money, and how, fearing that William Patrick's persistence would rake up the past and reveal that Hitler's father was illegitimate and possibly born of a Jewish girl, Frank was commissioned to investigate the family's ancestry.

There is no reason to doubt the authenticity of these memoirs, despite the fact that some details are certainly inaccurate. We must remember that Bridget was neither a politician nor a historian, but an Irish farm girl. Now that her memoirs are available in full – the only memoirs by any relation of Hitler – their merits can be properly debated and will no doubt be debated for years to come and no one has categorically proved that Adolf Hitler did not live in Liverpool from November 1912 to March 1913. Bridget Hitler has filled in what happened in the German dictator's missing year.

THE HITLER FAMILY TREE

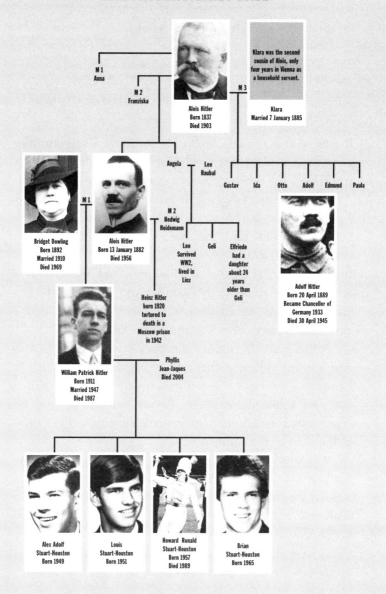

M 1
Anna

M 2
Franziska

Klara was the second cousin of Alois, only four years in Vienna as a household servant.

M 3

Alois Hitler
Born 1837
Died 1903

Klara
Married 7 January 1885

Angela

Leo Raubal

Gustav Ida Otto Adolf Edmund Paula

M 1

Bridget Dowling
Born 1892
Married 1910
Died 1969

Alois Hitler
Born 13 January 1882
Died 1956

M 2
Hedwig Heidemann

Leo Survived WW2, lived in Linz

Geli

Elfriede had a daughter about 24 years older than Geli

Adolf Hitler
Born 20 April 1889
Became Chancellor of Germany 1933
Died 30 April 1945

Heinz Hitler
born 1920 tortured to death in a Moscow prison in 1942

William Patrick Hitler
Born 1911
Married 1947
Died 1987

Phyllis
Jean-Jaques
Died 2004

Alex Adolf
Stuart-Houston
Born 1949

Louis
Stuart-Houston
Born 1951

Howard Ronald
Stuart-Houston
Born 1957
Died 1989

Brian
Stuart-Houston
Born 1965

MY BROTHER-IN-LAW ADOLF

By Bridget Hitler

1

It was at the annual Dublin Horse Show. Everyone had come to see and buy the fine Irish horses – English and Irish sportsmen, the nobility, tourists from all over the world.

I always enjoyed going anywhere with my father, and I must confess that I was not unaware of the honour of being escorted by "the best-looking fellow in the countryside", as he was generally described. Many eyes turned towards us: the tall Irishman and the girl in a white muslin dress with flounces and a blue sash. My white hat was ornamental with ostrich plumes, and I carried a parasol. This was the year 1909.

Father was discussing the horses with Mr Tynan, a neighbour, and presently they were talking with a handsome stranger dressed in a brown suit, a homburg hat and immaculate spats. To my interested eyes he represented the height of elegance according to the vogue at the start of the century.

A white ivory walking stick with a gold handle was hooked over his arm with inimitable dash. In his tie was a pearl pin, and two rings on his left little finger, one a diamond and one a ruby, added just the right note of lavishness. Across his cream-coloured waistcoat a heavy gold chain stretched from one pocket to the other and his moustaches were waxed and curled up right 'à la Kaiser'.

He introduced himself as Alois Hitler from Austria.

I cannot deny that this stranger, with his fine foreign manners and his debonair Viennese ways, made a great impression on me. His conversation was quite different from that of the commonplace hardworking farmers and their wives who made up the society I was accustomed to. Everything he said was so new and interesting that even his broken English seemed charming.

When the Horse Show was over we met in a Dublin museum in Merrion Square, and Alois invited me to tea. It was my first date with a man. Need I say that I was already head over heels in love?

My parents did not view our budding friendship with approval. Catholic and conservative, honest farmers for countless generations, they considered all strangers alien intruders. Consequently the idea of my becoming the wife of an Austrian, a foreigner, was decidedly repugnant to them. Their distress was aggravated by the fact that after my suitor had said that he was in the "hotel business" and on a European tour to study the industry in France, Belgium and the British Isles, my father, who had been suspicious from the start, learned that he was employed at the Shelbourne Hotel as a waiter, sent there by a London employment agency.

Finally, the situation became so unbearable that I had to choose between my family and my suitor. Perhaps I should have known better, but who could blame a seventeen-year-old for choosing the man she loved? We ran away to London without my parents' consent and were married there.

There was a great hue and cry at home after our elopement, and my father threatened to appeal to the police and have that "Austrian foreigner" arrested for a kidnapping, but he was dissuaded from doing so by my mother. It was not until a year later that I succeeded in making peace with my family, when father came to be present at the baptism of his first grandson.

We had named our baby William Patrick, but it was not long before I found myself calling him Pat. Alois, however, addressed him as Willie. Both of us clung stubbornly to our chosen nicknames. I am sure Alois never once forgot to say Willie, and it never occurred to me to call my baby anything but Pat. A little thing perhaps, but it might have served as a warning. How long can a marriage endure when the parents fail to agree on so simple an issue as the nickname of their only son?

Our marriage turned out very differently from the life Alois had pictured for me in such glowing terms, and it was very different too from life in my devout, industrious family.

Alois had a volatile Bohemian nature and was always just about to make a fortune. He changed his way of earning a living four times during our first two years of married life. From London we moved to Liverpool, where he opened a small restaurant in Dale Street; selling this, he bought a boarding house on Parliament Street, then a hotel on Mount Pleasant; then he went bankrupt and lost the hotel. There were times I didn't have enough money to buy milk for my baby.

One day Alois appeared, gay and smiling, "Cece, we are rich!" (he always called me 'Cece' after a portrait of St Cecilia which he particularly admired). Flinging a big roll of bills on to the table, he said he had won in the Grand National at Aintree. He scarcely gave me time to pack. Two hours later we were on our way to Le Touquet to play roulette. This was the first of many such trips;

whenever he had money we would go to the Continent –
Monte Carlo or other gambling places. On the way back,
having lost, Alois would always swear that he would
never go near a roulette table again, never again. But he
was a born gambler, only the lack of funds deterred him
from playing the races at Liverpool, gambling at cards,
anything that came along, and he was lucky sometimes;
then he was light-hearted and open-handed.

At such times he would send money to his sisters
Angela and Paula who lived in Vienna, with whom he
corresponded regularly. Angela, his older sister, was
married to a man named Leo Raubal, who held a position
in the Customs Bureau in Vienna. Paula, the younger,
lived with them. In the second year of our married life
Alois deserted his original profession, the hotel business,
to become a salesman of safety razors, which were a
novelty at that time. He began to dream of a great
international sales organisation, and planned to entrust a
central European branch to his brother-in-law.

In order to further this project Alois sent Leo Raubal
travelling expenses, so that he and Angela could come to
Liverpool. Alois had often spoken of Angela and I was
looking forward with pleasure to her visit. When we went
to Lime Street Station to meet them, I eagerly scanned the
couples descending from the 11.30 train, wondering if I
would recognise our relatives. Instead of Leo and Angela
Raubal, however, a shabby young man approached and
offered Alois his hand. It was my husband's younger
brother, Adolf, who came in their place.

Looking back now, it would be very satisfying to say
that my Irish second sight, or even my woman's intuition
had helped me recognise unusual qualities which might
explain why the young man we met would one day

become one of the most notorious figures in history, but there was certainly nothing about the pale, unsteady-eyed youth who began agitatedly whispering to Alois, that distinguished him from thousands of others.

One would have expected that for such a long journey he would have come fairly well-dressed. Certainly wearing such a worn-out suit could only mean he had nothing else.

Even so, I would have welcomed him as I would any member of my husband's family, had not Alois' angry voice startled me. He was furious. Forgetting his surroundings, he spoke so sharply and loudly that heads turned towards us in astonishment.

At first, Adolf, obviously exhausted from the long journey, mutely listened while Alois berated him, but then he replied even more heatedly. At the height of the discussion Adolf moved closer and grabbed Alois' top-coat by the lapels. For a second the tension was so great that I decided I'd better go; they had forgotten I was there anyway. I left them.

It was late in the evening when the brothers came home. We were living then at 102 Upper Stanhope Street, Princes Road, in a pleasant three-roomed flat. I settled Adolf in the room that had been made ready for the Raubals. I was annoyed with both of them for their untimeliness. The dinner I had spent hours concocting was completely ruined. Alois, who was an excellent cook, had taught me how to prepare his favourite dishes. This dinner was to have demonstrated to his sister my skill in Viennese cookery.

The moment they came in the room I realised that the earlier outburst had cleared the air between them, and now the two men sat down to the warmed-up dinner in a quiet, almost friendly mood. Adolf, however, was completely exhausted. His pallor and lassitude were so pronounced that I feared he was ill, and immediately after dinner he retired.

Alone with my husband, I reproached him for his unbrotherly behaviour, and for the scene he had made at the station. "I can understand," I told him, "that you were disappointed when Adolf appeared instead of Angela and her husband, but that doesn't excuse you for giving him such a rough reception."

When Alois spoke he smiled sarcastically, "You don't understand. If you knew everything, you'd feel as I do."

Alois had often spoken about his family before and had sometimes almost wept with self-pity at the way they had treated him. His earlier courtships and his aristocratic upbringing in Vienna were almost forgotten, though occasionally he would revert to them with the object of belittling me. Now all reserves were forgotten and he confided to me many details he had never before mentioned.

From the complicated family history my husband related I managed to make out that his father, also named Alois, had married three times. The first marriage was childless. My husband and his sister Angela were born of the second. Adolf, now sleeping in the drawing room, and his sister Paula were the children of the third marriage.

"I invited Angela and her husband to be our guests. I didn't invite that good-for-nothing Adolf. He's a disgrace to all of us. I want nothing to do with him."

His eyes clouded and his mouth took on the stubborn, twisted expression I knew so well. Whenever he spoke about his unhappy childhood, his upper lip would begin to quiver with emotion.

61

When Alois' mother died, his father had married for the third time. His new wife had from the start displayed a tendency to be a typical stepmother. When her children were born Alois' position became almost unbearable, and as he grew older it grew worse.

"When I was only thirteen," my husband told me, "my stepmother drove me out of the house. She persuaded my father to send me to Linz without a penny. I was apprenticed to an innkeeper, Herr Spressler. He was a brute. Three months later when my father finally came to see how I was getting on I had lost ten pounds and was black-and-blue from beatings. I threw myself on his knees and begged him to take me away. My father had always been stern with me, but I think he might have relented if it hadn't been for my stepmother. You see, I had always wanted to be an engineer, but that cost money. My stepmother needed all the available money for her favourite, Adolf, whom she kept at home. He hid behind her skirts, never doing a day's work or earning a *Heller*.

"Once I got into a serious scrape in Vienna. I was threatened with prison for being unable to account for a few crowns I had collected for my master. In desperation I asked for help, begging them to send me the missing crowns. I remember that exact words of the reply I got as though they had been engraved on my soul. 'To steal and to be caught means you are not even a good thief. In that case my advice is go hang yourself.' The letter was in Adolf's handwriting. I can never forget it, and I cannot forgive him, even though the letter was dictated by his mother."

I tried to calm my husband, for fear he would fly into one of his ungovernable rages. I had been aware for a long time that his childhood experiences had warped his whole outlook on life.

"There's no point in hating people on account of things so long past," I told him. "You're both men now. Your stepmother is dead. And after all, you and Adolf are both children of the same father."

My husband interrupted impatiently. "Of course we had the same father, but there are other reasons too, not just what happened when we were children. When my father died he left a house and a small piece of land. One fourth was to be mine. Do you know what Adolf did? After my stepmother died he sold that house and the land – my share too. We weren't children then. That was only three years ago. I wanted to charge him with embezzlement and send him to prison, but when I wrote to Angela from Paris – I was working there at the time – she persuaded me not to and he got away with that too." Alois was pacing back and forth as he spoke, and then he stopped before me. "Can you understand how he could have the cheek to come here, using the money I sent to Angela, after what he did to me? *Zum Teufel*, in his place I would rather have gone to jail, which is where he would have gone. The Viennese police had been after him for the last eighteen months."

Before, when Alois happened to mention Adolf, he had always referred to him in a patronising but also faintly sentimentally-masked manner as "my artist brother". Now that he was in a temper, he forgot entirely the grandiose distinction everything he described as 'my' usually took on, and disparaged our sleeping guest.

"When Adolf's mother died in December 1908 he went to Vienna and lived on our inheritance, mine as well as his. He had never learned a trade, so when the money ran out, instead of getting a job he just moved in on my sister Angela. He lived in her house and ate her food until even she got tired of it and made him leave. In the end he sank so low that he had to seek shelter in the Vienna municipal lodgings. Imagine how I felt when I heard that. What a disgrace! There's some excuse for old men who have nowhere to go and can't work, but Adolf was only twenty when he went there and he has stayed ever since. A man in his early twenties so shiftless that he lives in a lodging for old men at the city's expense! Isn't that shameful! And he's my brother."

"But you told me he was an artist." I wanted to stop him somehow. When he got so excited there was no telling what might happen.

"Cece, darling, don't be ridiculous. Artist! He's nothing but a cheap dauber. They wouldn't even accept him as a student in the Kunstakademie. And what kind of an artist is a man who copies pictures and signs them with his own name?"

"Is that why they want to put him in jail?"

"Oh no, something much more serious. He's a deserter from the army. You know, Cece, every man has to serve three years in the army in Austria. Adolf has been hiding from the military authorities, consequently from the police, for the last eighteen months. That's why he came here to me. He had no choice. When he confessed this at the station, he wondered I didn't welcome him with open arms."

It was easy enough for me to understand why my husband spoke so contemptuously about Adolf's conflict with the Austrian military authorities and police. No one could have been more careful in such matters than Alois; his papers were always meticulously in order and above reproach, lest he should get into disfavour with the authorities.

"In Vienna," my husband continued, "there is a rigid

system of registration of domicile. Within minutes they can locate anyone who fails to report for military service. Adolf knew this as well as anyone else. In order to evade capture he registered at the Vienna municipal lodging house under the name of his younger brother Edmund; Edmund was born five years after Adolf, and died at the age of two. By using Edmund's birth certificate he managed to identify himself as his younger and dead brother. That was how he dodged military service, living under the name of Edmund Hitler, while the Viennese police searched high and low for Adolf Hitler. When he was nearly cornered, Adolf threw himself on Angela's mercy, and she, poor soft-hearted woman, gave him the money I had sent for her and her husband to come and visit us. That was how Adolf got out of the country and saved his skin."

2

Before I go on to describe my brother-in-law's stay, I must interrupt myself with the following remarks.

Recently, during an interview in Washington, I was officially questioned about Adolf Hitler, and when I mentioned that he'd been in England the official immediately expressed surprise. "In what year did this visit take place?" he asked.

"It was 1912," I replied. "Although that's a long time ago, I can give you the exact date he came because it was only a few days after we took the flat in which we remained for several years."

"This is extremely interesting," he commented,

"because you are furnishing the answer to a very intriguing question."

He told me that there had been much speculation, by contemporary historians on the subject of a 'lost year' in Hitler's career. The year begins with the second half of 1912 and continues through the first part of 1913. Hitler, himself, in his autobiography, *Mein Kampf*, states that he left Vienna in May 1912 to go to Munich. In spite of the fact that this was supposed to be an official statement, it was false; all evidence shows that he arrived in Munich a year later than he claims. Conrad Haydn in his biography of Hitler, *Dear Sir*, gives the date of Hitler's arrival in Munich as 1913, as did Rudolf Olden, the famous German anti-Nazi writer whose book, *Hitler the Pawn*, was published in London in 1936.

Of course it's more than understandable why Adolf was so vague about this period. Certainly he would like it to be passed over as quickly as possible. When he wrote *Mein Kampf* he rearranged the facts of his early life into a more presentable version. To mention his trip to England without giving a reason for it would have been awkward, and the reasons would not have made good publicity for the German prophet. As for feeling grateful for the refuge granted him, it just wasn't in his make-up.

My brother-in-law Adolf remained with us from November 1912 until April 1913, and a less interesting or prepossessing house guest I cannot imagine. At first he remained in his room, sleeping or lying on the sofa he used as a bed most of the time. I had an idea that he was ill, his colour was so bad and his eyes looked so peculiar. I felt rather sorry for him, in spite of what Alois had told me. When I washed his shirt – he had no luggage with him – the collar was so frayed and worn that it wasn't even worth turning. I persuaded Alois to give him a few things, and as a matter of fact he wasn't at all reluctant to do so. Indeed I think he would have been more than willing to help Adolf if the latter hadn't been so unappreciative and difficult. Adolf took everything we did for granted and I'm sure would have remained indefinitely if he had had the slightest encouragement.

Thinking back, I found him only weak and spineless, but curiously enough I think he preferred my society to that of my husband. After the first few weeks he would often come and sit in my cosy little kitchen playing with my two-year-old baby, while I was preparing our meals. I thought he felt very much at home then. Usually he wouldn't say much, but just sit, from time to time telling me of the different dishes his mother used to make.

Sometimes he would speak of the future. It had been a great disappointment to him that he was not allowed to enter the Kunstakademie, where he had applied several times.

"The reason they gave for refusing me was that I didn't know how to paint, but if I could paint why should I go to the Academy? And that idiot of a professor," he complained, "said I had talent for architecture but not painting. I know that was only an excuse. He was prejudiced against me."

"But why don't you learn a trade, become an apprentice? I don't mean you should become a waiter like Alois, but you might take up something for which your interest in art might be helpful – photography, for example. Or do you really feel you have to be a painter?"

"Oh, I don't know," he replied uncertainly. "Up to now I always thought I had the ability to become a good painter. Maybe it's too late, as Alois always tells me," he sighed. "Maybe he's right. Of course, if I had another sort of brother, one who wasn't so selfish as Alois, he would give me enough money to live on for a few years while I developed myself."

This was one mood he displayed to me. Then there was another. In this respect he resembled my husband, but then they were always as much alike as two peas in a pod. Alois had maps of every country and was always studying them. When Adolf was with us I had to go through the same thing all over again. He would spread them out on tables, or even on the floor, and pore over them for hours, and he would never hesitate to interrupt my housework to explain how Germany was going to take its rightful position in the world. First would come France, then England. Naturally I didn't find this kind of talk very interesting, but whenever I tried to get away he would begin to shout, although I rarely troubled to contradict him. He would whip himself up into a rage and go on until hoarseness or some interruption stopped him. I put it down partly to the pleasure he took in hearing his own voice – another trick he had in common with my husband – and partly to a desire to domineer me.

As a matter of fact, I didn't pay a great deal of attention to his ravings. I suppose I was beginning to take shouting for granted as a family characteristic – and then, too, Alois' determined friends all talked the same way. I dare say this attitude was indicative of the general feeling of that time. Only occasionally did I retaliate. Once I couldn't stand Adolf for another minute and burst out: "You have a fine nerve coming here as you have and saying such things. You will never live to see the day England will be destroyed by Germany. If it ever comes to a fight, it's just as likely that the opposite will happen.

68

Anyway, why do you take such an interest? You and all of us too are Austrians, not Germans."

He stared at me as though I had struck him in the face. For a while he had nothing to say, but his bewilderment soon passed off, to be displaced by what I can only describe as a kind of sly pleasure in the fact that he had made a Britisher lose her temper.

When Alois had time, he took off to London. Adolf was enchanted by Tower Bridge, and they bribed their way into the engine room to see the immense machinery in motion. Alois had a regular passion for machinery and was pleased to have a companion on his jaunts. He showed Adolf power plants, dynamos, river cranes and the inside of ships. When they came home there would be endless discussions of what they had seen.

They both had an intense interest in anything English and were always going sightseeing. Though I don't mean to say they were storing up information for later use, certainly, at least sub-consciously, they were the forerunners of the tourists who later streamed out of Nazi Germany in all directions and brought home the odd bits of information which, patched together, formed a complete pattern.

I think it more than possible that Adolf's English visit gave him the idea. As soon as Adolf knew his way around he began disappearing by himself, not returning until late in the evening. He said he was looking for a job, but since he knew only a few words of English and never left early in the morning, it was always my opinion that he just wandered about Liverpool or went to stare at the River Mersey, or perhaps he spent his days in the taverns frequented by Germans.

One day he came back quite excited. "Listen Alois,"

he exclaimed. "They were playing the Bavarian National Anthem on the river. All the men took off their hats and stood at attention."

"That's ridiculous," commented Alois.

"No, no, there were many people there, and they all showed their respect." Adolf began to sing, *"Heil unserm König! Heil!"*

The moment Alois heard the tune he laughed. "You are crazy, Adolf. That's the English National Anthem. The music is the same. Only the words are different."

There is something else I should like to mention. I believe it was in my house that Adolf first came into contact with astrology. This subject had always interested me. I remember when I was a child, my mother used to talk to me about the planets. She told me that when you were born there are certain planets going over your head. Some are good, some are bad; they influence your whole life. I understood nothing but bothered her to tell me more. Since she didn't know any more, it was years before I satisfied my curiosity.

Not long before, I had met a Mrs Prentice, who cast horoscopes. My husband despised the idea, but from the moment Adolf first heard about it he kept after me for more details, though never in Alois' presence. He asked to have Mrs Prentice do his horoscope again and again. Years later, when my brother-in-law had become famous, there was much comment on his dealing with an astrologist; it was said he never did anything without first ascertaining the astrological aspects. I thought back then to the idle words I had spoken which had served as an introduction to this absorbing interest.

One day Mrs Prentice cast a horoscope for Pat. He would go to Germany, she predicted, and would be taught German. I didn't pay very much attention at the time, but it is curious that her prediction came true.

Tiring of Adolf's presence, Alois suggested he should go to America and even went so far as to offer to pay for his steamship ticket. At first Adolf was enthusiastic, but in a few weeks his interest languished. Adolf argued that he must learn English first, for without it he would be unable to make a living in an English-speaking country.

Alois countered that if thousands and thousands of Germans went there without knowing the language Adolf could too. Adolf agreed to go if Alois would advance him enough money to live on until he could support himself. That was more than Alois could have done, even if he wanted to, so the project fell through.

As the visit lengthened, relations between the two brothers became more and more strained. Naturally our family life suffered. Quarters were so cramped it was very difficult for me, and I had my baby to care for.

It is always easy to say "Tell him to go", but however absurd it may sound there was no way of getting rid of Adolf. He had moved in as a permanent guest.

Time and time again I have tried to think what qualities in the young man I knew then enabled him to make his later career. Actually the only striking personal attribute that comes to my mind is his incredible persistence. He knew we wanted him to leave – my husband even offered to pay for his room in an hotel – yet he managed to stay on.

"First I must learn English," he had said, but he learnt nothing, although he was always reading – not books, little pamphlets printed in German. These were Adolf's books. I didn't know what was in them, nor exactly where they came from, so I presume he must have got them from the Germans he met around the city.

Alois grew more and more impatient with him, but how could he deal with the situation? As a matter of fact there wasn't much he could do except be unpleasant, and when he would lose his temper Adolf would repeat, "You can't expect me to leave until I can make my own way. Surely that's not too much to ask of a brother."

After months of this Alois had an idea. He would inform our unwanted guest that we were giving up our apartment and moving away from Liverpool. "But what can I do then?" Adolf demanded.

The accumulated fury raging in Alois for the past months found vent in his retort: "What can you do? A young man of almost twenty-four years asks that? When I was your age I was managing more than twenty people in the Ritz in Paris, in third place after the director of the hotel, and you ask me what you can do? Well, I don't care. As far as I am concerned, you can do as you like. Go and hang yourself, as you told me when I asked for help."

His words ended in an almost hysterical shriek, but being a man of sudden impulses, ten minutes later he took out his wallet. This gesture between the two brothers was the equivalent to the signing of a peace treaty.

Alois bought Adolf a ticket to Germany. There was no alternative. During his Liverpool stay Adolf hadn't even picked up enough English to ask directions at the station. He had to go to a country where the people used the language spoken in Austria. He could not return to his own country, for he would have been arrested. Germany seemed the safest asylum because my husband found out by inquiry at the German consulate in London that there was no danger that Adolf would be extradited from the Kaiser's empire. They informed him that Germany did not extradite political or military refugees from Austria, even if asked.

Next day the brothers spent selecting the German city in which Adolf should attempt to establish himself. Adolf was unacquainted with Germany, but Alois knew it well, having worked as a waiter in several cities, and he advised Adolf to go to Munich because it was in every way – scenery, food, manner of dressing, customs and particularly language – the most like their own Austria.

At this point I pause to ask myself a question. Should I have been more sympathetic to Adolf? Would it have made any difference in the course of events, when Adolf was in Liverpool? I was young and thoughtless. Certainly I didn't concern myself with his future. If I had exerted my influence over him, it is quite possible he might have remained in England. At this time the country was full of Germans. Barbers, hairdressers, carpenters, all varieties of skilled workmen came looking for work. Many of these visitors settled comfortably in England, never to return to the continent. If I had insisted that Adolf learn English, instead of practising my stumbling German on him, he might have shared their obscurity.

As I think back to his departure, I see again the pale thin face and haggard eyes of my young brother-in-law, as he hastily kissed me and Alois before he boarded the train. Leaning far out of the window as the train began to pull slowly past the station, he shouted something ending *"zukunft wirst du Erstatten von mir erhalten."*

I looked at my husband in amazement, for I couldn't understand why he suddenly turned red in the face and started forward as if he wanted to run after the moving train.

"What's wrong?" I asked. "He only said you'd get what he owed you."

73

"Yes, that's what he said, but it had a double sense. He meant to threaten me, saying I'd get what was coming to me. But what do I care for the threats of a loafer like him?"

Who could have predicted that this 'loafer' would one day hold my husband's, my own, my son's life – indeed the life of all Europe – in his hands?

The end of 1913 was the beginning of our troubles, which continued until our marriage was interrupted by the First World War.

The razor business, in which my husband had been engaged for some time, did not turn out well. In fact, it was a failure. At least, it was a failure as far as he was concerned, for he had to withdraw from the firm; and when he fiddled for his share, instead of the millions he had been dreaming of, all he got was a few pounds. Yet this setback did not alter his ways.

In May 1914 he announced that he was leaving for the Continent and described with eager enthusiasm how he was going to make a fortune. It had been a mistake, he explained, to attempt to launch an English razor on the Continent. He would start a company in Germany. The German people were patriotic and would be much more likely to buy a German product than an English.

I didn't believe a word of it. I thought he was going to play roulette. He had what he thought was an infallible system.

"Haven't you found out yet that you can't win?" I protested.

"Why, Cece, I'm not going to play. This is business. It's a wonderful opportunity to make a fortune, you know."

It was useless to argue.

He left, and a week later I got a postcard from him. It

was mailed from Berlin. Of course that didn't prove anything – not that he was in Berlin at any rate. When I used to go with him to Monte Carlo or the other gambling places, he didn't like his business associates to know where he was. He would often have his letters sent from Berlin. He used the Paris/Irish firm which, for a small fee, would mail communications for its clients from anywhere they designated. I used to write to him care of them, as it was convenient to have a fixed address when he was travelling about.

The last card I received from him was also postmarked Berlin. The date was 28 July 1914. This is what he said: *Everyone is talking about war. They say it will break out in the near future. I don't believe it, but I'll be on my way back to England next week.*

But during the next week war broke out. If my husband left for England when he said he was going to he must have found the frontiers closed. Or perhaps he never meant to leave.

The war was on. He was in one world, I in another, and the frontier between us was guarded by millions of soldiers.

3

For the duration it was utterly impossible for me to make contact with my husband. Nevertheless I was confident that Alois would survive the terrible holocaust. He was so resourceful I was sure he would be able to find a safe berth.

When the war was over at last, I tried to get in touch with him. Soon after the Armistice was signed, all who had relatives and friends on the Continent 'otherside' made efforts to locate them. I wrote to the Irish agency, for that had been the last address he gave me. My letter was returned with a notation 'Addressee unknown'.

I also wrote to my sister-in-law, Angela, at her old address, and after a time she replied. She was living in Vienna with her three children and younger sister Paula. Life was very hard. She knew nothing of either of her brothers, having lost contact at the beginning of the war. She also informed me that her husband, Leo Raubal, had been killed in the war, perhaps her brothers had shared the same fate, though it might turn out that they were only prisoners.

I didn't give up hope. It had been announced that some half-million Austrian soldiers were still in Russian hands as prisoners-of-war. Many of them had not yet returned, due to the revolutionary conditions in that country. Perhaps, as Angela suggested, my husband and Adolf were among them. Little information reached us from that part of the world, none about prisoners-of-war.

There wasn't much I could do but wait for word from him. Of course, if Alois was all right he probably would have little difficulty finding me. A letter sent to my address before the war would reach me, because my parents had now moved over to Liverpool from Ireland and bought the eight-roomed house in which I had previously been living. Pat and I shared it with them.

Then the tragic news came that made any further search for Alois pointless.

In the spring of 1920 I went one evening to Edelweisshaus, a restaurant that Alois and I had frequented. One of the waiters, a former employee of my husband's, told me that he had been waiting for a long time for me to come in. He took a folded letter from his wallet, telling me it was from another German waiter named Erhardt Ernst, who had written from Germany and asked him to get in touch with me. The letter related that my husband had suffered a serious wound early in the war, and had been hospitalised for months. Ernst and he had been in adjoining beds, and each had agreed to carry messages for the other in case either failed to recover. Ernst had been the one to whom this grim duty fell and he was anxious to execute it. He begged his friend to get in touch with me and tell me.

Unfortunately, he wrote, *Mrs Hitler will not even have the sad satisfaction of visiting his grave, for the hospital where he died is in the Ukraine. The Bolsheviks are in control. There is revolution.*

Actually this news brought no material change in my own or my son's life, as since my husband's departure I had been living like other war widows, working and keeping things going as well as I could.

My situation, however, was much worse than that of other women in England who had lost their husbands in the war. I was married to an Austrian, a man who had fallen fighting England, or at least her allies. I didn't receive a widow's allowance or other privileges.

As a young girl my great desire had been to go on the stage, but I couldn't do any more than dream because my conservative family did not think it suitable. They had no objection, however, to my singing in the Dublin choir, and when I was married, although Pat took most of my time, Alois, who was musical himself, encouraged me to keep up with my singing lessons. For three years I studied with the Mayfair School of Music, under Mr Gregory Hast and Sir Landon Ronald. Now that Pat was no longer a baby, and my family less reluctant, there was no reason why I shouldn't realise my youthful dream, and that was exactly what I did. I played in comedies and revues. I toured with Harry Lauder's company.

One of the tours took me to the Continent. We played in Holland, Belgium and finally France: Lyons, Nice, and then Monte Carlo. That was where I saw my husband. I was in the chorus on the brilliantly lighted stage. Although the audience was in darkness I could see the faces of the people in the first few rows. Suddenly it was as though everything disappeared, except the face of one man. It was Alois, older and heavier, his moustache cropped smaller, but unquestionably my husband. He was sitting in the second row with a woman of a rather Mongolian cast of features, with slanting eyes and dark hair. He had recognised me at almost the same instant. Before I realised what was happening, he whispered something to his companion. Then they both rose and left.

The shock was so overpowering that I had no idea how I failed to give the least outward sign of it. The only explanation that occurs to me is that I was so well drilled in my part that I did it mechanically, without the slightest thought or pause. And anyway, no one had the faintest idea that anything had happened. It wasn't until I was back in the dressing room with the girls that I began to react, that I began to shiver as though I had taken a chill. And it was only then that I had time to think. There was no possibility that I could have made a mistake in identity, for if it had been merely a stranger who resembled Alois, why should he have got up and gone out? Yes, certainly it was Alois. And the woman with him, was she my successor? I thought of the many times Alois had brought me to Monte Carlo, when he was still in love with me.

Had I believed that my husband was dead? Or had I subconsciously felt that he would turn up one day? Almost against my will I realised that I had never believed he was dead. What a curious thing, then, that now that I was sure he was alive, for the first time he became dead to me.

Well, that was what he wanted, wasn't it? That was what he meant me to think. And that message from the waiter, why hadn't it struck me at the time that it was odd that a careless young waiter should go to so much trouble to send me a message? I saw clearly now that it had all been planned. Alois had sent me the message. I remembered how he had said I couldn't visit the grave even if I wanted to, because it was in the Ukraine.

A wave of fury swept over me. What a rotten thing to do! What a grim joke to play on one's wife! All right, if he wanted to be dead, so far as I was concerned he could be dead.

As I look back, there is only one thing that troubles me. I didn't tell Pat. He was such a sincere, serious boy I knew it would hurt him terribly to learn that the lost father he loved was just an unfeeling man trying to evade the responsibilities of marriage.

Pat was very grown-up for his ten years, and I know he regarded me as much too young to be taken seriously as a mother. In fact, we more or less grew up together. The question of his father was practically the only one on which I ever deceived him, and I wish now I hadn't. It would have saved both of us a great deal of pain and trouble.

As the years passed, Pat was developing wonderfully. He was in the boarding school at Ashford and was everything I could have wished. He was an earnest member of the boy scouts. His teachers praised him. He had written an essay which not only took first prize but was read before the assembled school. He showed definite artistic talent and had a keen imagination. I was very proud of him.

Naturally, in common with all children who have lost their fathers, he conjured up larger than life-sized pictures of him, trying to recall favourably significant things he had glimpsed as a child. In Pat's affectionate view, this selfish, thoughtless man had become a hero.

Mothers are not always as intelligent as they should be about their children. Instead of telling him the cold facts of our relationship, I spoke of Alois as little as possible, thus leaving a blank canvas on which Pat's imagination could work. One curious fact escaped me entirely – Pat's instinct that his father was alive and would return one day.

This happened in November 1923. After an absence of a few months, I went to my son's school in Ashford to visit him. Pat, proud as punch, showed me a newspaper containing an account of an unsuccessful coup d'état which had taken place in Munich. It was the famous Munich putsch organised by Adolf Hitler which had taken the military authorities twenty-four hours to suppress. Adolf Hitler, Pat was insisting, must be his uncle.

I took the newspaper in my hand. I looked at the photo. Adolf's face had become more mature and somewhat fuller; otherwise there was no great change except for his moustache. When Adolf had come to visit us in Liverpool his moustache had been of the handlebar type, rather full and soft. Long before that I had persuaded Alois to cut off the waxed points of his 'à la Kaiser'. When Adolf came, I set to work on him too and succeeded in getting him to trim it. Now I said that it had decreased still more, almost to a ridiculous degree. Alois' moustache had grown narrower too when I saw him in Monte Carol; it looked much better than Adolf's. I had started them in the right direction, but Adolf had gone too far.

I read an account of what had happened since he left England. When the war started he had entered the German army, where he became Gefreiter, the equivalent of a lance-corporal. At the conclusion of the war he joined a political party, later becoming its leader. When his beer-hall putsch turned out to be a fiasco he was arrested; now he was to be tried for treason.

Pat brought out his own treasured photograph album and displayed a photograph: Alois stood with his arm on Adolf's shoulder. It had been taken in one of their sightseeing tours in London. As they stood in front of the photographer, they appeared to be loving brothers. Pat compared this old photograph with that in the newspaper. "They're exactly the same," he said, "and I'm sure Uncle Adolf will answer my letter."

I looked at him amazed and inexplicably disturbed. "Your letter?"

"Well, I wrote a letter to the Mayor of Munich asking him to get in touch with my Uncle Adolf Hitler and tell him that we, his brother's widow and son, are living here and that he should inform us of all the details of my father's death in the war, and where he is buried so that when I'm older I can go there."

I didn't know what to say. His desire to know all about his father was so natural that I could find neither heart nor courage to tell him the truth. I prayed his letter would never reach Adolf.

Fate decided otherwise. There was a reply, but it was not from Adolf.

Dear Madam, it read, *it has come to my notice that you have been making enquiries for me, and I beg of you to state what it is that you want of me.* It was signed 'Alois Hitler' and came from Hamburg.

This was all I needed to set my Irish temper ablaze, and I wrote back that I wanted nothing from him, but that I felt he owed something more to his son than the cold response elicited by his inquiry.

The reply I received from my husband was undoubtedly the strangest piece of writing I had ever read.

A storm had been unleashed by Pat's innocent inquiry. By chance the letter had come into the hands of an officious member of the Munich municipal authorities who, whether moved by pity for the deserted mother and child, or by the desire to harm Adolf, had instigated an official investigation in connection with the allegedly dead brother of the Munich putsch leader. The investigation disclosed that my husband not only was not dead, but on the contrary had 'married' a certain Hedwig Heidemann and was living with her and a child born of their illegal union. As soon as he was in possession of the fact, the conscientious official had succeeded in having Alois charged with bigamy.

With a curious mixture of naïve candidness and cold cynicism Alois told me what had prompted him to write to me after ten years of silence. He had been called to the office of the Lord Mayor of Hamburg, for questioning. I quote: *I then denied nothing but gave a statement to this effect, with the exception that I don't regard this marriage to be legal, because it is not registered at the Austrian consulate. This statement I had to sign. Police sent the statement to the public prosecutor at Hamburg, and he threw in information from the Austrian consul as to the legality of the marriage. The*

82

Austrian consul declared that it did not matter to the legality whether the marriage was registered or not. The marriage is therefore to be regarded as legal. This declaration, as well as my own statement, was the basis upon which the public prosecutor won the charge of bigamy against me. My solicitor told me that now the only chance to clear me is to have our marriage legally dissolved before the trial of bigamy comes on. It is the only way to save me from the worst, by you doing me this favour. If you deny this to me, then the future will prove to you that you have been doing wrong. It is not only for my benefit, but for yours and Willie's as well. I also want to remind you of one fact. Don't think that I am at present a rich man, for to tell you the truth I am not. But I have got the chance to get rich by the aid of my brother's reputation. This chance will be lost for ever if I am found guilty, and if I get sentenced.

The letter now took on a new and different tone, saying that he had believed Willie and I were dead, eagerly assuring me of his eternal devotion over and over again. Of course, there wasn't a word to explain why he had got his friend Ernst to send me a message that he had died in the Ukraine. Nor did he indicate in any way on what he had based the belief that he claimed that Pat and I were no longer among the living. Neither did he explain why he had not made the slightest effort to find out what had become of us, or why, if I was really the great love of his life, he had scurried away when he recognised me in Monte Carlo. I wondered if the woman I had seen was Hedwig; she had looked Slavic rather than German.

Then the letter went on: *You must help me or they'll put me in jail. This bigamy charge is mainly embarrassing, for should the newspapers learn about it they're going to use it against my brother, who, as you must have heard, is the leader of the German political party which has missed reaching the top only by a hair's breadth. Although he is in difficulties now, he has by no means given up. When he is successful, I shall be in a position to compensate you for everything and could recompense you for all the expenses you have had in bringing up our boy and educating him. Up to now I could not share these expenses with you, for I have been living in very poor circumstances.*

The last pages of the letter deal exclusively with Pat, who he still calls 'Willie'. One passage runs: *Certainly I'll always stand up for the little darling boy, who once was in the sole possession of all my affection. And it is quite as you say. This poor little chap with his lovely, lovely blue eyes and fair hair, of which I still have some in my possession, is a victim of unfortunate circumstance.*

I sat at the dining-room table, at the home Pat and I shared with my parents. It was almost dark by the time I had waded through the contents of the letter, and I still remained there staring into the air absorbed and puzzled. What ought I to do now? I put the question to myself again and again, considering how I might spare my son the disclosure of this distasteful scandal.

At this point Pat came into the room. He needed only a glance at my face to sense that the pages lying in front of me on the table must have been the cause of my distress.

"Bad news?" he asked, looking at the letter.

I had no will to deceive Pat anymore, or even to take the letter from his hand when he picked it up.

Struck by the signature, he turned a puzzled face towards me and asked, "Is my father alive? Was this letter written by him?"

I stood up then and went out without answering. My heart was too full to speak. I left my son alone with the father he had found at last.

An hour passed before Pat came out, holding the

letter in his hand. When I had left him in the dining room with his father's letter he was an innocent thirteen-year-old boy, but now as he stood there before me looking at me with stony suffering eyes, he seemed to have grown into a man in that hour.

"Tell me, Mother, did you know my father was alive?"

"Yes, I did, son."

"But why didn't you tell me?"

"I didn't want you to have anything to do with a man who deserted you and for ten years didn't take the slightest interest in what happened to you or me. I wanted to save you from disappointment and disillusionment."

Pat shook his head. His face shadowed with disbelief. "Maybe he really did think we were dead. England was bombed by the Zeppelins. After all we had some narrow escapes. Maybe someone told him we were killed in the raids."

I knew the struggle that was going on in my son's soul. My poor boy, whose cherished dream had suddenly come true, was trying to hold on to it, not wanting to give up the father he had just found.

After this first communication from my husband, I was literally bombarded with letters from him. Adolf was mentioned in many of them. Alois had evidently experienced a change of heart towards his brother, as may be seen from the following letter.

Concerning my brother Adolf, I'll write you a letter shortly. Only one thing I'll tell you today about him. The reason you don't hear anything about him now is because they keep him captured in the castle at Landsberg in Bavaria. On 18 February starts a big trial, and then I am sure you will hear again enough of him. I would recommend you to follow up the reports about him then. One thing is sure to be, he will get out of it and win his battle easy and in honour.

Most of the romantically flowery letters had only one object, to persuade me to get our marriage dissolved in some way, perhaps by claiming I was a minor when it had been performed. Or that I had signed my father's name to consent.

"In that case," he wrote in one of his letters, "it is true that Willie will be an illegitimate child temporarily, but that shouldn't worry you, for after the conclusion of the case I am willing to adopt him."

Of course my being a Catholic made the whole affair doubly difficult, not to mention distasteful.

Alois's letters grew more and more desperate. One concluded: 'This I tell you, that they will not get me into prison alive.'

Not so much for myself as for my son, I felt I could do nothing but hold my position, that if either of the marriages was to be erased from the record it should be the second. Certainly that was the one that would be considered null and void by law, and by right, in any civilised country.

Eventually a legal separation was effected. Although we could not be divorced in the eyes of the church, that didn't disturb Alois. Anyway, Adolf was going to institute reforms in the field of marriage, Alois informed me.

Nothing about the affair ever became public. The court took into consideration the deposition I sent to Hamburg, requesting that my husband should not be punished for his offence since he had believed that my son and I had been killed in the raids and was consequently innocent of any wilful wrongdoing. Accepting this plea in principle, the court fined Alois the minimum amount, 800 Reichs-marks, without loss of civil rights. Contrary to reports, Alois did not go to prison, but received instead a sentence practically equivalent to actual acquittal.

After the trial was over, I received a letter from my husband thanking me for loyally standing by him, and predicting that Adolf would soon be 'on top'.

In later letters Adolf, to whom Alois now referred as 'uncrowned king of Bavaria', was a favourite topic. Adolf was going to do this. Adolf was going to do that. Adolf had written a book called *Mein Kampf*. I would hear about it. To me they sounded just like the old stories of how Alois was going to make a fortune, but one great plan for the future grew out of the other, and at least Alois was showing some interest in his son when he wrote: *Furthermore, in England he will always be a young man like millions of others, but in Germany he will be one of the only descendants representative of the man who bears the most prominent name of the present generation of Germany.*

It is my intention to put Willie in a position to enable him to make provision for you in days to come. Willie with his excellent character is well aware of the fact that in our complicated case it is his duty to do so. I, therefore, propose to him to come over here in the course of next summer. In the meantime he must learn as much German as possible, for it is important that he be able to talk at least a bit.

Letter followed letter. Several times Alois had invited Pat to visit him, but it was not until 1929 when my son was eighteen years old that he met his father.

At that time, 1929, Germany was fleetingly a modern democracy, the so-called Weimar Republic. The National Socialist party was slowly becoming the most important in the country, and the eyes of the world were focusing on its leader, Adolf Hitler. The English newspaper-reading public evinced intense interest in the activities and personal history of the rising politician. They wanted to know everything about his family, his origin and his past. Munich, the obvious source of information, refused to publish any details concerning the person of the leader, restricting their releases to purely official propaganda material. It was only natural, therefore, that the moment the newspaper disclosed that a sister-in-law and a nephew of Adolf Hitler were living in London where we had moved, public attention turned towards us from all directions.

I really couldn't say whether it was the newspapers which first blew our sorry status, or whether my son or I myself unintentionally made known the fact that we were 'related' to Adolf Hitler. Suffice it to say that from that time on we were a constantly recurring sensation in the London papers – which presented us as a special delicacy in the way of piquant 'reading material'. Whenever Hitler did or said something startling, the London newspapers sought out my son, asking for statements about his uncle.

Although Pat was only eighteen, he was employed by an engineering firm in Wigmore Street, in London. An old friend of ours, Mr JE Barrow, secretary and chief accountant, recommended him for the position.

Naturally Pat was greatly impressed by the fact that his uncle had reached such a high position in the world. To me it seemed incredible. I asked myself over and over again, what could have happened to the German people that an insignificant man like Adolf, whom I had known as an unwanted and disagreeable guest, should have been chosen as their leader. Where was this man going to 'lead' that people?

4

In August 1929, Pat was to have a two-week vacation. He proposed to use his holiday to comply with his father's urgent request that he visit him in Berlin. With eager anticipation he made all arrangements for the journey. I thought of Mrs Prentice, whose astrological forecast had predicted this trip so many years before. Certainly her insistence that Pat learn German had influenced me towards encouraging it, and now that he was going to Germany would the future bring the great things she prophesied were in store for him? I let him go, extracting a promise that he would write everything that happened to him.

I still have those letters, preserved with his first years and a lock of his baby hair. As I am preparing this manuscript and reread them, I sincerely feel that they warrant inclusion. An English boy, four years before the German dictator came to power, sets down in a frank account intended only for the eyes of his mother his experiences in the Hitler household. The first letter concerns his father:

Dear Mother,
The trip seemed terribly long, I was so anxious to get here, though I must confess after the train crossed the German frontier I wasn't so sure it was a good idea. All I could think of was those stories about the Kaiser they used to tell when we were children.

When I saw the signs 'Berlin Bahnhof Weinbergstrasse' my heart jumped right in my throat. I was going to meet Father. I got out and waited on the

*platform. I heard someone call me, "Willie, Willie,"
and the next minute Father rushed forward and
embraced me.*

*"You didn't know me," he was laughing, "but I
recognised you right away."*

*He grabbed all my luggage and rushed me to a
street car, talking every minute. He was in a great hurry
to take me home, and have me meet his wife and my
half-brother.*

*They live on the Luckenwalderstrasse in a third-
floor flat. You wouldn't like it – too much furniture and
too many pictures. Right on the most prominent spot in
the living room is a life-size painting of Uncle Adolf in
stormtrooper's uniform.*

*Father introduced me to his wife, whom he calls
'Maimee'. She said I had better call her that too. She was
very nice to me and seems very devoted to Father, but
it's easy to see that he's the boss of the household. She
hardly says a word when he is around.*

*Heinz is eight years old and very blond. I can't seem
to believe that he and I have the same father. I don't
think he looks anything like me, and it's so strange to
hear a voice speaking nothing but German, but Father is
trying to teach him English. Father always speaks
English to me when we're alone. I feel very strange here,
particularly with Father, though he acts as if he'd been
with me every day of my life. I had no idea it would be
so odd to be in a foreign country. I miss you very much.*

*After we ate a heavy dinner, Father brought out a
bottle of wine and poured out a glass for himself and
another for me. Then he settled down to talk about you.
"I can't get your mother off my mind. She'll always
remain the great love of my life," he began, but I didn't*

give him much encouragement. Then he took out his old-fashioned gold watch, opened the back of it and showed me a lock of hair. "Your mother's," he said, and quickly put it away again. I didn't like any of this very much, but I guess you want to know, so I'm trying to put down exactly what he told me. "My dear boy," he said, "I'm going to tell you our lives run in circles. If we do a good deed or a bad deed it follows up, or we come round and meet it. God has exacted a terrible punishment from me, for the way I treated your mother. She is a wonderful woman and no one realises it better than I."

That's what Father said about you and he made a big fuss over me too.

Well, goodbye for now, and take good care of yourself while I'm gone.

Your loving son, Pat.

Another letter concerned the first time Pat encountered his busy uncle:

Dear Mother,

I am writing you from Nuremberg, where we arrived yesterday. First thing in the morning Father greeted me with, "We're going to Nuremberg". I didn't mean to be impolite, but I didn't quite understand why he was so excited until Maimee explained. "Don't you understand? We're going to the National Socialist Party Congress, we're going to see Adolf."

Really, Mother, I think she was more thrilled than Father.

Father, Maimee, Heinz and I were on the train all day. It was frightfully hot. We rode in the third-class compartment, and for dinner we had only sandwiches and coffee Maimee had brought.

I had heard a lot about Nuremberg, and looked forward to seeing it almost as much as Uncle Adolf, but actually I saw nothing but flags. They were hanging everywhere, draped over everything. You couldn't even see the houses. It was like a gigantic country fair.

We didn't stay at a hotel. Rooms were at a premium since most of them had been reserved months ahead. We all crowded into a three-roomed flat of a friend of Father's. I heard Uncle Adolf make a speech in the Luitpoldhain, a large park outside the city.

There must have been about 30,000 men there, all in SS or SA uniforms, just like soldiers. I asked Father how that could be, and he said it was because Uncle Adolf was so clever. In the German republican constitution, he said, you can't find one word that forbids men to wear uniforms for a show like this. Father says Uncle Adolf is a genius because he does everything legally, and the Republicans who let him get away with it, Father said, have only themselves to blame because they are so weak and stupid.

Father went to speak with Uncle Adolf, telling us all to stay where we were. We were hoping to get a chance to talk to him too, but Father came back and said it was impossible as Uncle Adolf didn't want to mix his family with business.

The letter ends here and I received no more that trip. When Pat's holiday was over he came home full of excitement. It took him hours to tell me about it. He described the whole family in detail. Maimee had been very nice to him, and so had Alois's sister, Angela.

Angela had come to visit Maimee while Pat was there, so he had an opportunity to meet her and her daughter Geli, who was only a few years older than Pat, but he didn't meet her two other children, Leo and Friedl, until later.

Among the souvenirs of Pat's second trip to Germany, which took place in 1930, I found a letter which described the first meeting with his famous uncle. Here it is:

Dear Mother,

We had just finished dinner last night, and Father was unfolding the evening paper, when the bell rang. Heinz ran to open the door. It was Uncle Adolf, wearing a trench coat with the collar turned up and a homburg hat pulled down in front. Underneath he was wearing an ordinary blue business suit. He looks much better than in uniform.

Father was very surprised because the newspaper had said there was a big party meeting that night. "What happened?" he asked Uncle Adolf. "Why are you alone?"

Uncle Adolf was smiling, and jokingly said he'd got bored with the meeting and his bodyguards, and wanted some of Maimee's good coffee. "Anyhow," he added, looking at me with a twinkle in his eye, "I wanted to meet this Englishman."

Maimee quickly introduced me, then went out for coffee and whipped cream.

Father was quite excited at the honour of being visited by Uncle Adolf and began to walk up and down the room the way he does. Uncle Adolf sat down on the sofa under the oil painting of himself.

When Maimee came back with a large plateful of homemade cake, Uncle Adolf fell to and ate most of it. He seemed to be in a good humour and asked Father if he'd heard his latest speeches. I know Father was familiar with them because he'd been reading them to me out of the papers, translating the words I didn't know, but he listened very attentively while Uncle Adolf told what he'd said.

I had no idea Father could be such a good listener. Uncle Adolf didn't seem to be disturbed at all by my presence and told us all the news about Angela and her daughter Geli. You remember I told you about meeting them last year. Geli is the nicest of the whole family, and she can speak English too.

Uncle Adolf complained to Father about his troubles with the industrialists, particularly Herr Thyssen whom he had been visiting. "I have to keep on good terms with him," he said. "After all, the party needs their millions." He says that the "Jew press" is attacking him again, and the others all nodded their heads as though they knew what that meant.

Uncle Adolf had been looking at me from time to time as though he were curious about me. Now he turned to me and said: "And you, you English boy, what is your opinion on the Jewish question? What are they doing about it in England?"

I was really embarrassed but tried to tell him as well as I could in my broken German that we didn't have any Jewish question in England, and that we didn't make any distinction about religion. I told him we had many friends whose religion we didn't even know.

"In Germany it would be different," he shouted at me. "Germany is too small for religion and the Party.

The Party needs the whole man, not a piece of him. The Party must be everything to him. Even his family must be subordinated. That is how we shall build a strong nation. There will be no place for religion in the future. First we will get rid of the Jews. They are the weakest. And then we must rule out Catholicism. The Catholics are too well-organised. In a few generations no one will know that a Jew called Jesus ever existed, and no German will be ruled by a man in a robe. Germany will be our religion." And then he wound up with: "Germany is chained, thanks to the Jews and the Catholics."

"I am a Catholic," I told him.

"I know," he said, "and so am I. But it's true just the same. Catholics drove the dagger into Bismarck's back, and it doesn't matter what country they live in, they all stick together. But Germany must be German first. We must make sure of that."

I felt like pointing out that he was an Austrian himself, but thought better of it and contented myself with asking him, "What about the Protestants?"

I guess he had been a little bit hard on the Catholics then, because he suddenly slapped me on the back and laughed loudly saying, "The Protestants are not organised." Then he asked me jokingly if I went to church every Sunday.

When I said I did, he and Father both laughed. Then Father said, "I never found going to church paid my rent."

It was getting late then, so Uncle Adolf had to go. Another letter is devoted to Pat's cousin Geli, I include it because it bears almost unique witness to that odd love story between uncle and niece, which culminated in a mysterious tragedy.

Dear Mother,

Yesterday Aunt Angela and Geli came for a visit. It's the first time I've seen Geli this year, and I was glad she came, because we always got on well.

You know, Mother, Geli looks more like a child than a girl, though she's actually older than I. You couldn't call her pretty exactly, but she has great natural charm. She's just a nice height, not too short and not too tall. She has deep blue eyes and blond wavy hair. She usually goes without a hat and wears very plain clothes, pleated skirts and white blouses. No jewellery, except a gold swastika given her by Uncle Adolf, whom she calls Uncle Alf. She told me her name is actually Angelica, but Uncle Adolf nicknamed her Geli and gradually everyone has taken it up.

We made a date for today. Geli loves to walk, and offered to show me her favourite haunts in Berlin.

I went to call for her at the Gasthof Ascanischer, the hotel where she and Aunt Angela always stop when they come to Berlin. Usually they live in Munich. The hotel is pretty rundown and shabby. You'd really think they might choose a better one. When I said something about it to Geli she just smiled. "You don't know Uncle Alf, Willie!" Like all the family, she calls me Willie. "He wants us to set an example of frugality to the people. He never permits us to spend a penny more than is necessary."

As we strolled through the city, Geli kept returning to the topic of Uncle Adolf. He seems to be very much on her mind. She was very young, when she and her mother went to live with Uncle Adolf. Geli's father died in the war, so Uncle Adolf acted father to her and the other two children.

"He was utterly strict," she told me, "though more with the others than with me. He was always different with me. I am his special favourite. He would never go to sleep without saying goodnight to me, even when he didn't get home until long after I was in bed. Lots of times he would wake me up in the middle of the night just to say a few words."

I guess Geli is the only one Uncle Adolf is affectionate with. She told me even when he's in a savage mood, storming about and breaking things, if she begins to cry he pulls himself out of it and comforts her.

There were long periods when she scarcely saw him at all. He had no time for anyone when he was fighting for the life of his party.

That was when Geli began to study music seriously. She has a fine natural soprano voice, and her teachers say she could be a success in opera if she would really devote all her time to it. But Uncle Adolf doesn't want Geli to have a career. He thinks she should learn to be a good housewife first. In fact, I don't think he approves of careers for women at all.

She said only once did he lose his temper with her. That was one night when she was out late after a concert and a boy brought her home. Uncle Adolf was furious and forbade her to go out with boys at all. It was a week before he was nice to her again, and then he began to take her everywhere with him. They would go riding in his car. When he was in Munich, Geli stayed at his Prinzregentenstrasse apartment. He even took her on party business to Berlin and

Nuremberg. They were inseparable.

I guess if it weren't for Geli's music she probably would allow herself to be completely enslaved by him, for that's what his interest actually amounts to. He wants to take absolute possession of her. He can't bear to have her show the slightest interest in anything or anyone other than himself. Any moment she must be ready to go where he wants, stop whatever she's doing to follow his slightest whim. Sometimes he makes her sit at the movies all day with him, then go back in the evening. Geli gets bored but has to accompany him. She never quarrels with him, but it's only necessary for her to try to get out of going to make him angry. There is never any time for her signing lessons. "I think he's jealous of my music," Geli said.

After we talked awhile I found that it wasn't so much the music Uncle Adolf objected to as Geli's teacher, who comes especially from Vienna to give her lessons. He's half-Jewish, and Uncle Adolf doesn't want Geli to have anything to do with him for that reason.

That seems daft to me. As Geli said, "What difference can his being Jewish make? He's a fine teacher." Uncle Adolf is really hipped on the subject. Geli says she can't even talk to him about it.

It's quite a problem for her, because she feels she owes Uncle Adolf a lot for bringing her up and taking care of her mother, and she's sure he's really fond of her, but she doesn't like it that he watches her all the time and doesn't let her do anything she wants.

I asked her what she wanted to do, and she said, "Go to Vienna and study singing." She told me sometimes she feels like running away. Anything would be better than being kept down the way she is.

She was practically in tears this evening and very upset about the whole thing.

I didn't know what to tell her. She has a very nice voice, but if Uncle Adolf was against her, it would be difficult for her to do anything with it, and of course she has no money except what he gives her. Anyway, I think it's too bad.

Well, this is much longer than I intended and it's late, so I'll close.

With love, Pat.

When Pat came home we had a long talk and I asked him what the family thought about Adolf and Geli.

Maimee thoroughly disapproved and said it was ridiculous that Adolf should behave as he did, taking Geli everywhere, and holding her hand and kissing her and cuddling. She said Geli was a sweet girl and it was a pity Adolf wouldn't leave her alone.

5

One day we received a letter from Alois which, innocent enough in itself, had remarkable consequences. I quote from it as follows: *By reading the English papers I have seen what a lot of nonsense these papers serve to the public, and it can only be for the good if this nonsense gets corrected by an authentic statement. A paper wrote for instance: 'He fought in Cuba against the Spaniard and he fought against England in South Africa' etc. What a nonsense! At the time of the Boer war, 1899 to 1902, Adolf Hitler (born 20.4.1889) was twelve years of age. I therefore give you the following instructions. The brief story of Adolf Hitler which I sent you last year contains all important dates and actions of Adolf, and I authorise you to utilise the copyright of this entire pamphlet, but don't give it away for nothing. Any further inquiries you can direct to me by giving them my card, which I enclose.*

Alois was right. At that time the English press – and also the American, I presume – was full of fantastically garbled stories about Hitler. Since Adolf Hitler had previously been a nobody and could not be looked up in *Who's Who* there was no source of precise information available to reporters. Consequently they simply made up stories or repeated gossip they had heard.

We decided to present our account of his 'real life story' to two journalists we knew, Mr Bliss of the *Evening Standard* and Mr Frank Long of the *Evening News*. The resulting article was correct in every detail.

After its publication we forgot about it and went on working as usual.

A telegram arrived. We had no reason to connect it in any way with the article which had appeared in the *Evening Standard* and *Evening News*. The telegram was as follows:

FATHER DYING STOP COME BERLIN AT
ONCE STOP AUNT ANGELA.

The wire had arrived in the morning. There was no question as to whether Pat should go or not. He left for Berlin that night. The following day I expected a message from him, but none came. I told myself it was because his father was dying and Pat couldn't leave his bedside, though it was unlike Pat not to keep in touch with me.

Six days later Pat came back from Berlin. Contrary to custom, he didn't notify me beforehand of his arrival. My first glimpse of him was anything but reassuring. His face was pale and drawn, and there were dark circles under his eyes.

"My father wanted to see me," he explained. "That's why he sent the message. He took me to see Uncle Adolf." His voice petered out and he looked at the ceiling, his expression troubled. I knew Pat wasn't telling everything. It's difficult to deceive a mother, especially when her son has been as close to her as mine had always been. I knew he was trying to spare me by keeping back something that was worrying him.

"Why don't you tell me, Pat? Maybe you'll feel better," I urged him. "You know you can tell me anything. What happened?"

"You're right, Mother, and I do want to tell you everything, though it's not easy. It was a great disillusionment. The first shock was when I got off the train in Berlin. Father was standing on the platform, when I had thought he was dying. I was so surprised I couldn't speak, and you know, Mother, I would have liked to turn round right then. How could he let Aunt Angela send me a telegram that he was dying when there was nothing the matter with him? All the way from London to Berlin I'd been praying that I would get there in time to find him alive, and there he was as healthy as I am. There wasn't anything wrong with him at all. 'You must forgive me, Willie,' he immediately began to explain. 'Adolf insisted on my sending you the wire. He wants to see you.' He looked at me and I could see he was wondering how much he ought to tell me. Then he said: 'Adolf is furious, and I hope to God that you and I get out of this without becoming a head shorter.'"

Pat couldn't believe his father meant what he said seriously. His uncle was an important man, he knew, but that didn't give him life-and-death power over his relatives. An automobile was waiting for them. Angela was in it.

"What has happened?" Pat asked, as soon as they were in the car. But Angela and Alois made it clear that they couldn't talk in front of the driver. Pat didn't get a word out of them.

They pulled up at the Hotel Kurfürstenhof, a second-class hotel on the Linkstrasse. Pat said it looked more like the headquarters of an army than an hotel. He was astonished at the spectacle before him. Uniformed soldiers were rushing about saluting snappily. Perfect discipline obtained. Pat remembered what his father had told him about Adolf's soldiers. Yes, decidedly, a man who could maintain a private army might very easily be in a position to shorten a few necks.

They went upstairs and waited outside Adolf's door. More and more people came in and went out and there were always telephones ringing. Pat thought their turn would never come. Finally, a young man came out with a basket full of letters and spoke to Alois who introduced him to Pat. It was Adolf's private secretary, Mr Rudolf Hess. He immediately greeted Pat in English, and said they could go in.

Adolf, dressed in a business suit, was standing at the middle of one of three enormous windows, looking down on to the street, not letting on that he had even noticed their entrance.

It was a big corner room, furnished only with a large desk and a few chairs. Angela sat down. Alois and Pat remained standing.

Adolf turned round and glared at the three of them, and then began to walk nervously up and down the room. This must have gone on for several minutes before he pulled up sharply and shouted, "To me, exactly to me, this has to happen."

But instead of explaining, he started off again raging up and down, mumbling to himself, to the blank walls, to the air, to anything except his relatives. "I am surrounded by idiots. Yes, you, you are idiots. You're tearing down everything I have built up with my own two hands."

Adolf's hair was tumbling over his forehead, but this time he didn't bother to fling it back. His arms flailed the air in wild violence. He turned to Alois. "You criminal. You succeeded in smashing everything."

"But Adolf …"Angela tried to reason with him. But he didn't pay any attention.

"What did you tell the newspapers?" he rasped at Pat. "Who gave you permission to appoint yourself an authority on my private affairs?"

This was so unexpected Pat didn't know what to say, but Alois immediately tried to defend him, by saying he knew nothing, they hadn't told him.

"Then tell him now," Adolf roared, turning his back on Pat.

Alois explained that two days before, the New York office of the Hearst papers had called up the Braunhaus in Munich and demanded to speak to Adolf Hitler personally. They wanted to know if he had a nephew in London who was an authority on the Hitler family.

Adolf furiously interrupted. "They put personal questions to me, to *me*."

Pat still couldn't grasp why Adolf was so angry. After all Alois had asked us to correct a false impression created by the English journalists. Pat thought he was doing Adolf a favour.

Why didn't Alois explain?

But Adolf had only begun. "My personal affairs are being discussed. Anyone can say who I am, where I was born, what my family does for a living. They mustn't learn about this stupid bigamy. I can't have it. No one must drag my private affairs into the newspapers. I never have said one word they can use, and now this happens."

"I don't understand anything," Pat said to his father. "I didn't tell anything except the truth, as you …"

"The truth!" yelled Adolf, nearly beside himself. "The truth! I'm being attacked from every side. I have to stand before them without the slightest stain, the slightest blemish. The shadow of a suspicion would be enough to ruin me." His voice faltered. "Can't you understand that? Or are you too stupid? I am surrounded by fools. My own family is destroying me."

His voice trailed off almost into nothing as he allowed himself to sink into a chair, his hands lifting to hide his face. "I have been so careful. I am only a step from attaining the top. I might even become Chancellor. And now there is a 'nephew' to tell them all the miserable little details they want to know. They'll hound me."

At this moment the door opened to admit an SA officer carrying a briefcase.

Adolf looked round and thundered at him with a violence Pat wouldn't have believed possible. "How dare you come in here? I left orders not to be disturbed. Get out, out!"

The astonished intruder gone, Adolf again dropped into the chair. Grasping the edge of the desk, he began to sob. His eyes brimmed with tears and he cried out choking: "Idiots, idiots! You will destroy everything. You will ruin me, you." As though tortured beyond human capacity to endure, he rose painfully and gasped hoarsely: "I'll kill myself. I'll put a gun to my head." And he lurched out of the room through another doorway.

Stunned by what had happened, bewildered by the situation, Pat turned to Angela. "But what harm did I do by telling the truth?"

"What was the title of the article?" she asked.

"My Uncle Adolf!"

"It's not true," Angela cut in, looking sharply at Alois. "Even if your father said so in his letters, you'd better understand once and for all that it's not true. Your father isn't related to Adolf, so naturally you aren't either. Your father had a different father and a different mother. He just lived in our family as an adopted child. By rights he is no Hitler at all and has no justification for using the name."

"Is that true, Father?" Pat asked Alois.

"Yes, that is so."

A few minutes later Adolf returned. He was in complete control of himself, and came directly to Pat. "I know none of this is your fault, but you must help me put things to rights."

Angela took advantage of this new mood to plead: "You are right, Adolf. After all the boy is innocent. He didn't understand he was doing anything wrong when he told the newspaper reporters he was related to you. Now that he sees things clearly, I am sure he will be willing to return to put things right by telling the newspapers he was misinformed, and that he was mistaken in claiming relationship with you."

"Yes," agreed Adolf. "That's the only way to proceed." He offered Pat his hand, and spoke in a very sincere, serious tone. "Will you go back to London and make amends for this, even though it wasn't really your fault but your father's? He should have told you the truth long ago."

Adolf sat down on the top of his desk and they all looked at Pat. "When you get back to England, I presume the reporters will get in touch with you. All you have to do is tell them you made a mistake."

"A mistake?" Pat asked.

"Of course. You were mistaken when you thought you were my nephew. You misunderstood your father. Or perhaps it would be best to tell the truth – that he lied to you."

His sudden contemptuous glance flicked towards Alois, who had seemed on the verge of protesting. "Yes, better tell them that your father lied to you. Now he had admitted to you that we aren't related at all, the reporters will let you alone if you tell them that."

"I'll be in a rotten jam," Pat said to him. "They'll think I'm a fake."

"I know I am asking a great deal," he said, "but I'm sure you want to do the right thing. I should consider it a great favour."

Pat had concluded his account and sat staring in front of him. I wondered if it was true that there was no blood kinship between my husband and Adolf. It seemed impossible to me. While I had been living with my husband, I had ample opportunity to learn the mystery of the Hitler family, its origins and complexities, and now I vividly recalled the bitter words my husband had uttered at the time Adolf was our guest in Liverpool. If there was no blood kinship between them my husband would surely have mentioned it then, and would have thrown it up at his brother on every occasion, and there had been plenty of occasions when he would have found sufficient provocation.

It was clear to me that they had staged a comedy to deceive my son. They had intimidated my husband so that he too had to take part in their scheme, which had undoubtedly originated in Adolf's brain.

Eventually it had become irksome to Adolf that there was an English boy who could call himself his nephew, and an Irishwoman who was his sister-in-law. If Adolf should deny it himself no one would be convinced. That was why he had lured my son to Germany. That was why they had tricked him into agreeing to confess he was an impostor. A young, inexperienced boy could easily be imposed upon, and the public would certainly believe him if he should come forward and deny his own words. Another thing too might have motivated Adolf. This was his hatred for the brother who had caused him annoyance and embarrassment with his bigamous marriage and who had been so reluctant to assist him when he had been in trouble in Liverpool. Perhaps he had welcomed his chance to humiliate him.

I came to the conclusion that if it was inconvenient for Adolf Hitler to have an English relative at large it was just as inconvenient for that English boy to have an uncle like Adolf. Besides, it might one day become a fatal circumstance to have him for an uncle, particularly as he might not always be allowed to carry on his activities unmolested. At least, that's how things looked to me that day. It would be best for Pat to sever everything that bound him to a man of that sort.

"Yes, Pat," I told my son. "It's not only Adolf. Your father's sister Angela and your father say the same thing.

There's nothing left for you to do but accept the situation and act accordingly. And I would advise you to tell the newspapermen who want to write about you that your relationship with Adolf is a mistake. I would even go a step further and advise you to change your name. Surely an English court would permit you to rid yourself of a name that is a handicap to you. They would readily understand that you don't enjoy being called Hitler."

When Pat didn't answer at once I studied his face for a long time. What was going on in his mind? How was he taking this disillusionment and chagrin? What effect would it have on him? The most talked-of man in the world was now forcing my son to demean himself before his own countrymen, to deny what he had honestly asserted. And they way he had been cajoled and bullied into making his promise, how must he feel about that? When I questioned him gently, his reply was serious and considered.

"Don't worry, Mother. My whole opinion of my uncle has changed anyway. Since I saw him as he is I don't want him for an uncle. In fact, I don't want to have anything to do with him, particularly as Geli died under such peculiar circumstances."

This was the first time I knew that Geli, about whom Pat had so often spoken, was dead. "But when? How? I never heard anything about it?"

"Nor I. Perhaps I never would have heard anything about it, except by accident. When we were leaving Adolf's office, Aunt Angela shook her head and said, 'Poor Adolf. He is suffering terribly. He wouldn't have taken this so badly if he wasn't so unhappy about Geli's death.'

"Naturally my reaction was the same as yours just now. All Aunt Angela said was that Geli had died very suddenly three months before, on 18 September. Geli was dead. I couldn't believe it at first – a young healthy girl my own age. 'An accident,' my father explained as we were waiting for the elevator. 'You mean a suicide,' Angela corrected him sharply. Curious that one should say one thing and the other another, I felt there was some mystery about it. I had no opportunity to question my father on the subject, but later in the afternoon, when I was alone with Maimee, I got her to tell me all she knew."

Maimee, so quiet when Alois was around, was always ready to talk in his absence. From the beginning of their acquaintanceship, Pat had found her a willing dispenser of intimate details on all topics relating to the family. This occasion was no exception.

In spite of the fact that she had been sincerely fond of Geli, who was, from all I heard, an exceptionally warm-hearted and lovable girl, Maimee allowed her desire to gossip full play and reported all she knew and had heard about the affair, which included not only what Alois and Angela had told her, but also certain details she had obtained through conversations with the housekeeper.

"Angela, Adolf and Geli," Maimee told Pat, "were having dinner at the Prinzregentenstrasse apartment in Munich on 17 September. As they were eating, Geli, said calmly, "I should like to go to Vienna, Uncle Alf."

Adolf had looked at her quickly. "Why should you go to Vienna? What do they have there you don't have here?" He was beginning their many-times repeated discussion, which always ended in tears for Geli.

But Geli, though her voice was trembling, quietly insisted. "Dear Uncle Alf, I must go to Vienna for a little while."

Realising Geli wasn't going to be talked down, Adolf's attitude changed to one of hurt resentment. "But why? Why do you want to go?"

"I want to see Aunt Paula."

Adolf pushed aside his plate and sat staring at the tablecloth. Minutes crawled by, but the silence continued. Finally Adolf stood up and began shouting. "We're getting to the bottom of this right now. You say you have to go to Vienna. Is it to see that filthy Jew, the one who claims to be a singing teacher? Is that it? Have you been seeing him secretly again? Have you forgotten I forbade you to have anything to do with him? Tell me the truth now. Why do you want to go to Vienna?"

Geli looked up into the tortured face of the man who was in love with her. "I have to go to Vienna, Uncle Alf, because I'm going to have a baby."

Completely stunned, Adolf had stared fixedly at his niece. It was some time before he spoke, in a voice like a two-edged knife, cutting himself even as he hurt her. "That's just fine, wonderful. Perhaps I should congratulate you." Geli began to sob, the unexpected storm burst over her head, issuing in a torrent of questions. "It's that scoundrel of a Jew. How could you do this to me? How long has this been going on? Why wasn't I told before?"

Geli could not answer, only sat weeping as Adolf flung the questions at her all over again. He gripped her shoulders and squeezed them as though to force a response from her. Still she remained mute. Suddenly Adolf picked up his riding whip, which happened to be lying on a chair with his hat, and went menacingly towards Geli. Aunt Angela screamed and took the whip from him, and then led him to a chair, in which he sank, completely unnerved. Staring now at Geli, now in front of him, he repeatedly shook his head, as though unable to comprehend.

110

After a long time, he got to his feet and went to Geli, who hadn't uttered a word since her confession. Adolf gently placed his arm around her shoulder and said in a low tortured voice: "Please don't worry. We'll find some way out. I'm terribly nervous, but I'll be all right soon. Then we can decide what to do."

Angela, relieved that the storm was over, and knowing that Adolf was leaving on a tour starting from Hamburg, proposed that the whole question be settled on Adolf's return. To this Adolf agreed and went to his room to get ready for the trip, which was scheduled to last for about a week.

Angela thought she should return to Berchtesgaden, where she was in charge, and asked Geli to go with her that night, but Geli insisted on remaining in Munich. Angela left at about five in the evening and subsequently was not in the apartment when the tragedy occurred.

The story of what happened during the next hour was told later to Angela and Maimee by the housekeeper, Josephine Bauer, the only witness. For a while after Angela left there was quiet, and then the shouting began again. Why or how, no one will ever know. Fragments of sentences, the words "Father", "scandal" and then "I can shoot myself", repeated several times, were all that penetrated to the ears of the anxious woman who was washing the dishes after that unfinished meal. Suddenly there were running steps and the slam of a door; furniture was falling, and she was sure Adolf was beating Geli. She claimed to have heard the swish of a whip and Geli began to scream. Josephine Bauer screamed too in sympathy.

A short time later, Adolf was about to leave for Hamburg and was already sitting in his car, when Geli called down to him from her window. "Uncle Alf, I ask you once more. Will you let me go to Vienna?"

"No!" Adolf shouted back from the street. Then there was the muffled roar of the Mercedes starting, and he was gone.

Perhaps a quarter of an hour later Josephine Bauer entered the living room. As it was empty, she continued on through the other rooms until she came to Geli's. It was locked.

"Fräulein Geli, Fräulein Geli," she called.

Geli did not immediately answer. Then in a voice scarcely audible through the door she replied, "He's locked me in."

Josephine Bauer went to the kitchen for a bunch of keys, one of which fitted. Geli, lying on the bed, smiled briefly and murmured "Thanks", but refused any further assistance except to ask for a small box in which to bury the body of Honz, one of the four canaries given her by Adolf, which had died that day.

Next morning when Josephine Bauer arrived at seven, as usual, the apartment was full of men. Windows were closed and blinds drawn. Josephine Bauer was informed that Geli was dying and that she was to remain in the kitchen and keep quiet. The terrified woman could get no one to pay attention to her.

Shortly after seven Josephine Bauer telephoned Angela in Berchtesgaden, telling her that Geli was very sick, something terrible had happened.

It was ten in the morning when Angela arrived. The room was full of Adolf's friends. They told Angela that Adolf had received the news in the night and had returned shortly before Angela. He and Dr Brandt, an intimate friend, were with Geli.

As soon as Angela realised what had happened, she

rushed towards Geli's room, but was not allowed to enter. Beating on the door with her fists, she demanded to see her daughter, but was kept outside, although Geli lived for some hours more.

Only Adolf and Dr Brandt remained with the dying girl.

Suddenly the door opened. Adolf stood in the doorway, eyes bloodshot, face waxy pale, hair hanging in a matted tangle. Seeing his sister, he abruptly retreated towards Hermann Göring, who stood a short distance away, and collapsing against the latter's shoulders began to weep hysterically, saying, "She's dead! She's dead!"

Angela who had automatically started towards her daughter's room, when she saw Adolf come out, stood before him as though powerless to take another step.

"She's dead," Adolf cried, "and I am her murderer."

At these words Göring intervened. "You're upset, Adolf. You mustn't say a thing like that. Frau Raubal might misunderstand. Tell her the truth, that Geli committed suicide." He turned to Angela. "My Führer was not even here."

Göring's emphasis on the fact that Adolf was not present when Geli was shot became the keynote of Adolf's alibi. He wasn't there when it happened. According to the account Angela publicly gave of the fatal evening, Adolf left for Munich and then Geli committed suicide.

But people whispered that Adolf had come back, Maimee hinted to Pat. In fact, added Maimee, Angela once let slip something to that effect but quickly reverted to the official story. "Nobody knows," Maimee concluded "what really happened, except that Geli was shot."

This was the gist of the story Maimee told Pat. When

she had finished, he wanted to ask her some questions, but Maimee must have regretted having carried on to tell him so much, for she nervously asked him not to speak of it any more.

"I don't know what happened that night," Pat said to me in a troubled voice, "and I didn't have time to find out, but from what Maimee told me I don't see how it could have been a suicide. Adolf's departure and immediate return sounds wrong to me somehow, and if he came back that night he must have found Geli alone in the Prinzregentenstrasse flat, because Aunt Angela was in Berchtesgaden. God knows what might have happened between them. Poor Geli. Well, it's not my business, I suppose. She wasn't even my cousin. Anyway, my relationship with Adolf is finished, closed. I'd like to forget the whole thing."

6

I believe it was the very day Pat arrived from Germany that we first attempted to retract our earlier statement and make it clear that we had no connection with the family of the German Chancellor.

When I was alone I took down an enlarged and tinted photograph of Alois in my son's room and burned it in our tiny fireplace. I felt as though a weight was lifted from my heart. It was almost like a ceremony. I thought I had obliterated every tangible thing that connected me with that disreputable family. I was burning my past.

There was a brief statement in the morning paper, but

it didn't help. No one who hasn't gone through it can understand what innumerable annoyances and unlimited hours of bitterness those endlessly repeated newspaper articles caused us. Those who heard of the denial justly questioned: "Why did he say something a few weeks ago that you are constrained to deny today?"

Then there was another, a psychological consequence, of our about-face. When the first stories connecting us with Adolf Hitler appeared, many people doubted them, on the grounds that whenever a new public figure gains prominence there are always people who come forward and claim kinship with him. At that time they doubted the statement that we were related to Hitler. Now the very people who doubted the assertion found something suspicious in our refutation, even though we tried to make it plain that our first statement had been based on a misunderstanding. As a result of our denials, far from sinking into obscurity we shifted even more into the limelight. I blame myself for this.

Pat and I were both working for the same engineering company in Wigmore Street. One day Mr Caligari, the secretary, came to me and informed me that they were reducing the staff of my department. I was dismayed, but since I'd been the last to come I supposed I must be the first to go. But it struck me as odd that they paid me a week's salary in lieu of notice, and then the secretary added: "And I would advise your son to look for a new position also."

"Why, what has he done?" I asked surprised.

"Well, after you leave here, his life won't be worth living."

My son and I smiled wryly at the similarity of our experiences, and didn't take the coincidence too

115

seriously, thinking we'd both find new positions. But Mr Caligari's heartless words almost proved true. We were disappointed, and bitterly at that. Days and weeks passed. Like most working people we had laid aside something for a rainy day, and of course we got the unemployment dole, but now our savings were being swiftly consumed. Wherever my son applied, his handsome appearance and agreeable manners won him immediate attention, but as soon as his prospective employer noticed the name on his reference he would look perturbed and say almost invariably: "Oh, by the way, are you related to that German chap?"

"No, I'm not related to him," my son would reply.

"I thought I read something about it in the papers. Well, I'm sorry. We haven't got anything that would suit you at the present time, but we'll keep you name before us."

Week after week, coming home after a day spent in fruitless searching, we compared notes. Our daily adventures ran parallel. I had tried giving my maiden name, and once I succeeded in obtaining a position, but as soon as one of the papers I had to show disclosed my identity, I was given notice.

Our quest became more and more hopeless. At first we had supposed that after a few months people would forget us and we could sink into the quiet and unsensational obscurity of the average humdrum London existence, but ours was a special case.

And the prediction of my husband, that Hitler would reach the top, became reality. On 30 January Adolf became Chancellor of Germany.

Now whenever the dictator crossed the Rubicon and Germany had a bad dream, or caused someone else to have one (unfortunately things of the worst kind happened almost every week), the eyes of the world turned towards Germany. And the English victims of these recurring sensations were none other than ourselves.

In our minds a new idea was beginning to take shape. We would go to America. Why should we not follow the example of those millions who left their homes to try their luck in the New World? The more we thought about it, the more hopeful we became. We would dispose of all our possessions in England and take passage for a new life.

The end of May we arrived home to find a heavy yellow envelope, postmarked 'Wien' (Vienna). I hastily opened it. As I unfolded the sheets of papers we saw that they were birth certificates, death certificates and other family records.

Pat had gone for advice to a friend of his, Dr Brown, who was connected with the London Auto Club. With the kindest of intentions, but without consulting us, Dr Brown had approached the legal department of the Vienna British Embassy and requested them to secure for me the birth certificates of Adolf, Alois and their fathers. Dr Brown thought these would enable us to prove Pat was not related to the Hitler family. And thus the hindrance to unemployment would be removed. Of course, as I could have told Dr Brown, the documents from Vienna proved the opposite.

"Look here, Mother," Pat exclaimed holding out two of the documents, "there's Adolf's birth certificate and this one is my father's. Both of them have the same father – Alois Hitler, customs employee. So they lied to me when they said they had different fathers. It was a plot, by Angela, Adolf and my own father. What do you make of it?" And then Pat looked at me as though my face had suddenly become that of a stranger. "Oh, I see. You knew

117

all the time. You deceived me too."

"Don't be silly, Pat," I told him. "Naturally I knew, but I thought it would be better that way."

Pat's face blazed with anger. He flung the documents on the table and slammed out of the house. I think it was the only time in his life that he lost his temper with me. It was several hours before he came back.

The moment I saw his face, I knew he was himself again. Almost before he was through the door he was saying, "I wrote to Adolf, Mother, and I told him what I thought of him.

"To Adolf?"

"Yes, Mother, to Uncle Adolf, and I don't think he'll deposit my letter in the Berlin state archives. I told him I had documents which proved, beyond the slightest possibility of contradiction, that he and my father had the same father, and that I know now that he lied when he said I wasn't his nephew. And I told him how unfair I thought he'd been to place me in such an awkward position."

He stopped for a moment, thinking hard. Then he went on.

"I wrote another letter too, to Father. I don't know whether he'll approve of it or not. I think a son should respect his father no matter what he may have done. But a father has some duty towards his son too, and when I saw these papers I couldn't restrain myself from what a disillusionment it had been to me, when I found out he had Aunt Angela send the telegram saying that he was dying. I said I just couldn't understand him, and to learn that he had plotted against me with Uncle Adolf and Aunt Angela was too much. I told him it had been his duty to tell me the truth. He might have trusted me enough to tell my why I was being put into this

118

unpleasant position. Perhaps Adolf had some good reasons for not wanting to have English/Irish relatives. My own father might at least have confided in me. He had no reason to deceive me. At the end of my letter I told him you and I have decided to go to America. And, Mother," he added, "I mailed them right away so you'd have no time to object." Pat paused again, and then laughed gaily, as he does when he's pleased with himself. And as he spoke I felt proud I had a son who could leave disappointment behind and turn with debonair spirit toward the future.

A few days later Pat received a letter from his father, asking him to come to Germany for a 'family meeting'. Adolf was going to settle things. Pat decided not to reply.

Instead we accelerated our plans to make a clean break. Unfortunately, however, no matter how we cudgelled our brains to make our resources stretch, there was barely enough money to pay our initial expenses and none at all to carry us over the period we might have to wait before making desirable connections.

It was at this point that Alois telegraphed me from Berlin:

DON'T MAKE THE MISTAKE OF GOING TO AMERICA STOP YOUR AMERICA IS HERE IN GERMANY STOP COME HERE IMMEDIATELY AND I GUARANTEE IN 24 HOURS AFTER YOU ARRIVE STOP I WILL HAVE POSITIONS FOR YOU STOP GO TO THE GERMAN EMBASSY IN LONDON STOP THEY WILL PROVIDE YOU WITH FUNDS FOR THE TRIP STOP BRING WILLIE WITH YOU STOP

We read and reread the telegram, trying to decipher its meaning, hoping to find between the lines an answer to our question. We discussed and debated its contents until late in the night.

Pat felt he should go, but I protested vehemently. It wasn't that I didn't think he could get a job in Germany; we both had complete confidence in that part of the plan. No, I couldn't easily define the cause of the uneasiness that ceaselessly welled up from the bottom of my mind. I just felt I shouldn't let him go. As for the suggestion that I go, I didn't even consider it.

Pat, seeing an end to the long and hopeless months of unemployment, and the prospect of being able to earn enough money to ensure the success of our plan to go to America and start over again, grew so enthusiastic that he merely smiled at all my doubt and objections.

"Why should you imagine that anything could happen to me in Germany? It isn't as though I was going out there to become a German. I'm still English, and if you're worried that the Nazi germ might get into my system, why that's just impossible. Those few weeks I spent in Germany made me immune forever to that infection. Even if 'Uncle' Adolf himself should try to convert me."

We spent the next day in preparation for the journey, and the day after I accompanied Pat to the railroad station, to see him off.

"Don't worry, Mother," Pat said, trying to reassure me. Even though I hadn't said any more, he knew I was still troubled about his going. "I'll only stay until I can save enough money so we can do what we want. It won't be long – I can live on very little."

As the train rode irrevocably away, the apprehension

I had felt before took a new hold on me, and I couldn't shake it off. I should never have let him go, I repeated to myself over and over again, as I stared after the departing train, the hot tears blurring my eyes. The way home had never seemed so lonesome and gloomy before.

Pat was gone. I received a postcard from Strasburg, where his train stopped for a half hour. It was the only sign of life. A week passed with no word. I watched the papers. It was the commencement of the Nazi terror – cruelty, priests arrested, Jews being beaten, democrats assassinated: it was frightful. How could I have been so senseless as to let Pat go to that terrible country? Now it was too late, I prayed that nothing had happened to him, but how could I be sure?

After a second week had slipped away without my hearing one word from him, in response to the telegrams of inquiry I had sent, I went to the German Embassy.

"What's happened to my son?" I demanded of the first official I met. "He's a British subject and unless I receive satisfactory news of him …"

Trying to calm me the man asked, "What is your son's name, madam?"

When I told him, the official looked at me with great surprise. "Isn't there some mistake, madam? Is your son's name really Hitler?"

"There's no mistake," I replied emphatically. "My son is the nephew of Adolf Hitler. He left for Berlin more than two weeks ago, and I haven't heard from him since."

"But my dear madam," he smiled, "you can't for a moment suppose that anything could happen to the Führer's nephew. Please sit down. We'll call Berlin at once and find out."

Fifteen minutes later I heard my son's voice over the

telephone. "I'm all right, Mother," he was saying. "There's nothing wrong. I don't understand why you haven't heard from me."

Then a second voice interposed. It was that of my ex-husband. I recognised it the moment he said the first word.

"My darling Cece, there's no need to be anxious about Pat. He's right here with me. Why should you be worried? You ought to be ashamed for worrying for no reason at all."

I had heard my son's voice and it was therefore obvious that no harm had come to him. But I left the Embassy feeling inexplicably disturbed.

For a whole year I hadn't seen my son. Every week a letter or postcard arrived. I learned that he had a job in the Reichskreditbank in Berlin. As I write these lines the letters Pat sent me during his stay in Germany are lying before me on the desk. They are brief and cautious. Anyone could tell that he was aware of the fact that every line was being minutely examined by someone. It is amazing how much you can read from what isn't said in a letter.

Every letter commenced and ended with an apology for his not being able to send me any money. German wages were arranged to fall into certain categories, certain living-standard categories. Pat's were fixed at a level which enabled him to eat and keep a roof over his head, but that was about all. Yet in spite of his meagre salary, Pat had managed to save up a little money, only to find that the restrictions existing in Germany with regard to sending money out of the country made it impossible for him to send me even the small sum he had eked out for that purpose. And because of his name and family connections, he had more reason than other people to respect the law.

During the first year of his absence, in almost every letter there was some vague reference to the fact that all German workers are entitled to vacation and that he hoped nothing would stand in the way of his spending his vacation with me in London. By this time I had managed to obtain a suitable position there, but in his later letters I could read his bitter disappointment between the lines, which told me in a matter-of-fact way that all employees of his company had renounced their right to a vacation that year. Naturally he couldn't be the exception. With this my patience was at an end. On the spur of the moment I wrote to him, telling him to resign his job and come home as soon as possible. I told him conditions had greatly improved in England during his absence, and assured him he wouldn't have to roam the streets looking for a job because of his name any longer. One of his objects in going to Germany had been to help me. I no longer needed that help, which hadn't materialised anyway. I had a good place myself now, and it didn't make sense, because he couldn't take any money out of the country.

I received no reply to this letter. There was no official censorship at this time because Hitler was still affected by international opinion. However, all letters were opened by the currency inspection control, ostensibly to make sure that no money was sent out of the country, contrary to German regulations. Actually this was a disguised censorship, by means of which Hitler controlled correspondence with foreign countries. And unfavourable or inconvenient letters had a way of disappearing. In a later letter to Pat, I mentioned that this letter must have gone astray and again urged him to come home. In a brief note Pat replied that he couldn't think of returning home.

Apprehension and dismay filled my mind to the exclusion of every other consideration. I read and reread my son's letters, trying to decipher from them what was the true state of affairs.

Pat's letters contained nothing but reassurances, I was convinced that he was keeping from me everything that he would normally say. Could it be that he was doing this because of the danger involved in telling me the truth?

I decided to write to Alois, my ex-husband, and demand that he use his influence to help Pat get home. He replied according to his custom, in a long ardent letter, praising our son extravagantly, telling me how happy he was, what excellent company he kept, how inconsiderate of me it was to insist on his giving up a position which promised a great future and had started so proficiently. Then he said: *On the other hand, why couldn't you come here, Cece darling? If you are so anxious to see the boy, why not come and visit him? You could come by plane as far as Paris and then to Berlin. It's only a short trip. If you're willing, I'll be pleased to arrange it with the German Embassy in London, so that they facilitate your journey.*

Alois must have felt pretty sure of my reaction, for he didn't even wait for a reply. The following day I received a letter from a Mr Thorner, an official at the German Embassy, requesting me to come and see him. When I presented the letter I had received, Mr Thorner brought out a file and said, "I have received an order from the Chancellery to advance you funds for your travelling expenses, and to assist you in every way. When would you like to leave, madam?"

I replied almost automatically, "As soon as possible."

The moment the formalities were arranged, I sent Pat a telegram informing him I was coming, and at noon the next day I left London. I had just enough time to catch the train which took me to the Channel. After crossing the Channel and France I got off at the Bahnhof in Berlin at nine o'clock the following morning. The moment I left the train, I saw my son rushing to meet me. As he kissed and embraced me, he whispered into my ear, "Mother, you have done an insane thing in coming here. You shouldn't have come to Germany."

"Good Lord, tell me what's happened."

My pulse almost stopped as I waited for his answer. He was still holding me in his arms as he said, "We can't talk here. Don't say anything until we get to the hotel."

7

Fifteen minutes later I was sitting in my son's room. During the quarter of an hour it had taken to get home from the station I had learned more about present-day Germany than I could have from reading a thousand articles. Pat wouldn't permit me to talk to the porter who was carrying my luggage, for one couldn't be sure he wasn't an employee of the secret police. He insisted we keep quiet while the cab driver was in earshot. The hotel porter, the lift boy, the chambermaid – all were to be suspected of being spies. And when at last we were alone in his room Pat hung his jacket on the doorknob, so that it covered the keyhole, in case some informer might decide to use it. He began to speak as we sat on two chairs he had pushed close to the window.

"It was impossible to write anything, but now that you're here we'll have to do the best we can, and at least we have a chance to see each other. You can't imagine how I've been longing to see you."

As he was speaking I studied his face. It was colourless and drawn. I couldn't make up my mind what had caused this, the lack of proper food or the constant awareness of being watched, spied on.

"We may never have such a good chance to speak freely, so I want to tell you now," he said. "I haven't time to choose my words, so forgive me if I'm too rough and don't give you a chance to say a word."

I listened to him, trying to summon up my courage. From his manner and what he had already told me, I knew it was going to be pretty bad.

"Go on, Pat. You know me well enough to know that I can behave like a man when there's trouble."

After a little hesitation, Pat began to speak, "Perhaps I am mistaken. Perhaps we haven't as much cause for alarm as I have been thinking. It's difficult to keep a perspective in Germany – it's possible I see things blacker than they really are. One thing is certain, you and I are in a nasty position here, up to now the fact that I am English and you were in England was all that saved me."

"What do you mean, Pat?"

"I'd better tell you everything. Then you'll see my – and now your – situation, and can judge for yourself. To begin with there's the relationship between Uncle Adolf and me. We are on the worst possible terms. When I first came here he made all sorts of promises, even gave me money, and I had no trouble in finding a job, but although the Reichskreditbank was paying me 189 Marks a month, after all the deductions – taxes, insurance, contributions to six organisations – I actually received only 140 Marks ($50, £10). I could live on that in Berlin but with nothing left over. When I came here at Father's request, I was led to expect I could make a decent wage, not just barely exist. If I couldn't do more than pay for my own food the whole project was a failure.

The obvious course, Pat told me, was to look for a better-paying job, but no one can change positions in Germany without special consent. When he tried to discuss this with his father Alois was furious. No one would dare offer the Führer's nephew any kind of job, regardless of salary, high or low, unless Adolf was willing. And Alois forbade Pat to take any steps. He seemed to think Pat should be satisfied just to make a living, but Pat didn't take his orders. He wrote to Adolf and explained the situation to him. There was no answer. Next he wrote to Angela; she didn't answer either. Pat decided he would have to see Adolf in person to get any action. He went to the Chancellery. The ante-room was jammed – no luck. So he waited until late in the evening. Of course he could go only after business hours, so it was the same story the next time he went. He was unpleasantly surprised by the rudeness of the attendant – not to him, but to the others who were waiting, most of whom were men of standing. They must all have had important matters to discuss, or they would never have got that far; yet the SS men treated them like beggars. There was one man who sat there for hours, holding a heavy briefcase on his lap. Pat knew who he was. His picture had been in the papers hundreds of times. An important Rhineland industrialist, he'd been there since

11.00 in the morning, but kept waiting patiently. When opportunity offered, he merely stated that he had an appointment: the Führer had sent for him to go over certain plans – he would wait. When he began complaining mildly, one of the storm troopers planted himself in from of the man, who was old enough to have been his grandfather, and ordered him to leave. The old man stood up and started towards the door, but his measured steps evidently didn't satisfy the SS man, for he came up behind the old man and pushed to hurry him on. It wasn't so much the action itself. The shove wasn't very hard and the old man wasn't hurt. But the way he did it, grinning at his companions and sneering at the old man's embarrassment, was shocking.

Pat decided that it was no use trying to see Adolf that way. Instead he wrote to Adolf's personal adjutant, SA Gruppenführer Brückner, for an interview. In reply Pat received a letter asking him to come to his office.

"Have you heard anything about Schaub or Brückner in England, Mother?" Pat suddenly interrupted his narrative to ask.

"No," I replied. "Or a least nothing that didn't sound so exaggerated I couldn't credit it."

Pat looked at me oddly. "Nothing they could say about Uncle Adolf's guardian angel could be too exaggerated."

Herr Schaub, Pat told me, is the subject of much popular gossip because of his treatment of his sister, or rather half-sister, who is considered not quite Aryan. He has tormented her so much that she has gradually become a common barfly. At first she used to frequent the Likenstrasse night club, to drown her sorrows. Then she acted as the hostess, trading on her charms and her brother's name to stimulate business. But ever since he had thrown her out of a lodging house, because the landlord was Jewish, she'd been in such a low state, running after every chauffeur and mechanic who'd buy her a drink, that everyone had begun to wonder when she'd be the victim of one of those 'accidents', that had become so frequent. Brückner, said Pat, is a huge hulk of a man. He drives one of the most expensive cars in the country, given to him by Adolf. Makes you think of a modern centaur, half-man-half-car. You almost never see him without it, unless he's in a night club, or so drunk he can't drive. Then he leaves 'baby' – that's what he calls his Mercedes – in the street, because he can't bear to have anyone drive it.

These two men, I learned, are at Adolf's side day and night, and there isn't much choice between them. Schaub's a small man, shy and quiet; Brückner is coarse and domineering. Both are dangerous.

In spite of his grim reputation, SA Gruppenführer Brückner had always been decent enough to Pat before. But the moment he began to speak on this particular occasion Pat felt a definite hostility in his manner. Brückner didn't bother to get up or even offer Pat a chair. His tone was rough and impatient.

"I understand you wish to speak to the Führer?" he said. "What do you want to see him about?"

"I should like to have an interview with him," Pat said politely.

"Yes, I know. You would like to earn more money." Brückner laughed derisively. "As if we all wouldn't."

Pat told Brückner he had plenty of offers. All Pat needed was his uncle's consent, because without it no one would risk hiring him.

Brückner leaned forward slightly and shook his head,

"You have a suitable position now," he said coldly. "The Führer has executed his duty towards you and does not feel called upon to do anything more." He signed Pat's pass and pressed a button. The door opened. The interview was at an end.

After this rebuff Pat tried to figure out why Adolf wouldn't allow him to improve his circumstances. What was Adolf's objection in forcing him to continue on subsistence wages? Pat couldn't arrive at a satisfactory conclusion.

"I'm not sure I understand why," Pat said thoughtfully, "but the fact remains that Adolf has never done anything for his own family. On the contrary he has made sure they will remain in obscurity. He has been unable to rise with the circumstances, even being able to dispose of the lives of 67 million human beings hasn't been enough to sublimate his desire to tyrannise over his own family."

Pat's life, at this time, was divided sharply into two levels. During working hours he was an underpaid, underfed, overworked white-collar man, like millions of others. In the evening and on holidays he was sought after by everyone. At first he was charmed by Berlin's hospitality and more than glad to be wined and dined on a much more lavish scale than he could afford. But the motive soon became apparent – it was not as himself that they wanted his company, but as the Führer's nephew. Every host had some scheme to sell, some favour to ask. Naturally no one had an inkling of the true relationship between Pat and Adolf.

The whole situation seemed pointless and hopeless. Pat was stumped. Finally, he made his decision. He would go back to England. No matter how hard a time he might have there, it would be infinitely better than this, and he would be home.

The first person to whom Pat confided his intention was his employer, Herr Berlitz, the director of the Reichskredit-gesellschaft. This kind and sympathetic man was completely taken aback. "Does the Führer know?" was his first comment. When Pat shook his head, he said, "You must inform your uncle at once."

As Berlitz spoke, his manner had undergone a startling change: from the genial cordiality of a powerful executive it had become the nervous uncertainty of a worried underling. For the first time Pat realised how precarious the bank director's own position must be.

During the following days, Berlitz repeatedly asked Pat whether he had told his uncle. Had he seen him, or written?

Berlitz's continued solicitude had an effect he could not have anticipated. It spurred Pat to action, but of a sort which would have inspired Berlitz with the greatest misgivings had he known of it. His experience with Brückner having served as an object lesson as to the futility of indirection, Pat determined to conclude the whole affair and, with this object in mind, wrote a letter to Adolf, in which he not only said he was returning to England but poured out all the bitterness he had stored up for months. He would try to find work in England, and if he couldn't get it because of his name he would make a public declaration that he had nothing to do with Adolf Hitler, and wanted nothing to do with him.

"Pat," I interrupted him at this moment, "there's something I don't understand. Does Adolf admit you're his nephew now, after all the fuss earlier?"

"Oh, he glossed it over. First he told me not to speak

about it. Then he just sort of forgot the whole thing. Lots of people know, of course, that before he became Chancellor he was terrified of scandal, but the way things are now in this country it would be impossible for anyone to make a scandal. All the newspapers belong to him. Radio, even public opinion is directed by him. No, I'm no longer a problem, so far as his reputation is concerned. I had a talk with Rudolf Hess, Uncle Adolf's private secretary, on the subject. He made my position clear. Yes, it was true I was Adolf's nephew and I needn't deny it, but I mustn't take advantage of it either. I would be best, he told me, never to refer to it at all. So that's how it stands."

"I see. Well, what happened about the letter?"

The moment Pat put it into the box, he told me, he had misgivings. So it was hardly a surprise that there were immediate repercussions. Next day Gruppenführer Brückner, Adolf's adjutant, appeared at the bank to escort Pat to the Chancellery. Followed by the unconcealed envy of his fellow-employees, Pat stepped into Hitler's private car.

He had barely time to settle back before Brückner began to storm at him. "What arrogance, after all the Führer has done for you, to write him such a letter."

Pat had been more than ready to regret his rashness, but Brückner's stinging words acted as a spur to his temper. "I don't see why I should account to you for what I write to my uncle, Herr Brückner," was Pat's retort.

"Oh no, but have you no shame that you dared to attempt blackmail against the Führer?"

Pat was astonished and furious. "How dare you make such a charge against me?"

This outburst was evidently unexpected, for Brückner made no reply, but sat biting his lip. Then in a quite different tone, he said. "There will be no question of your leaving the country, until we know what you propose to tell the English press."

So that was it, Pat thought. They were afraid he might talk. He began to see his position more clearly. "I am an Englishman," he shouted, "and I defy the right of any German to tell me what I have to do. I'll leave Germany when I please, and I'll write what I want. If you have an objection, refer it to the English consul."

"Is this so?" Brückner laughed shortly, staring at Pat with raised eyebrows. "We will see about that. As a matter of fact, why do you want to leave?" he asked. "The whole Reich is at your disposal." When Pat made no reply, Brückner lapsed into silence saying nothing more until they arrived at the Chancellery.

Brückner left Pat waiting in the ante-room, while he went into Adolf's office. A quarter of an hour later he opened the door. "Now you can go in."

Adolf was alone in his inner office. He sat gazing at the top of his empty desk as Pat entered. "Heil." He looked at Pat and smiled.

"Heil," Pat replied. (You never say "Heil Hitler" when you go into Adolf's office. And anyway, Pat never did. It made him feel silly.)

Adolf presented a very worldly appearance on that occasion – dark blue suit, well-groomed hair, manicured nails, fresh-shaved with the powder still showing a little.

"Well, sit down, won't you?" he said ingratiatingly, as though it were a great pleasure to see Pat.

From his first word, the impression Pat received in the car with Brückner was strengthened. Adolf considered Pat's return to England a threat. It would be awkward to interfere with the rights of a British citizen. Pat determined to take advantage of this weapon

Brückner had inadvertently put into his hand.

"You wrote me a letter," Adolf began, "not a very courteous letter, you must admit."

"I grant it wasn't very courteous," Pat interrupted, "but after all, when I came to Germany I was promised I'd be able to make a living, and send something extra to my mother. Otherwise I would never have come. I know I could get a better job if you would consent. It seems quite clear now that I made a mistake. I can take a hint. I think it would be best if I return to England."

Obviously annoyed, Adolf began to speak, his tone conciliatory. "You have a job and you can maintain yourself on your earnings," he told Pat. "What more can you expect? I didn't become Chancellor for the benefit of my family. You must understand that a Chancellor is in a peculiar situation. I can't have people saying I show favouritism to my family. No one is going to climb on my back."

It was funny, Pat said, that all he could think of as Adolf was speaking, was his *mot* on Napoleon, who had put all his brothers in high positions.

Then Pat went on with his story. "I don't want to climb on anyone's back," he had retorted hotly. "I can stand on my own two feet, but why should so many obstacles be put in my way? And my mother's?"

"You keep talking about your mother," said Adolf, "but she is not too old to work. Why shouldn't she support herself? It's not as though I am in a position to do anything for her myself. You know I am not a rich man."

I had been listening to Pat's story without saying a word. Now I couldn't help breaking in. "Why, Pat, I don't want anything from Adolf. And anyway, I'm getting on without anyone's help."

"I know, Mother, but you don't understand. It's the

134

principle of the thing. Uncle Adolf claims to be the only statesman in the world without a bank account, but this is just another example of his hypocrisy. He not only has a personal bank account in the name of Birkenshaw, but he also has several million marks in a joint account with Schaub and Brückner, which he keeps in the Reichskreditgesellschaft, Director Berlitz told me. So you can imagine that his remark about not being rich rubbed me the wrong way. But it wouldn't have been clever to reveal my knowledge. I said, Yes, I knew he wasn't a rich man."

Pat's tone must have indicated something of his feelings, for Adolf's expression changed. He began to ruffle the papers on his desk. Picking up a sheet he said, "I've received a number of reports on you."

That was something of a jolt to Pat. Who could have been sending in reports on him?

Adolf replied to Pat's unasked question. "Director Berlitz reports on you every month, as we agreed when you were first employed there."

Pat doubted it. If Berlitz had been making monthly reports, Pat felt sure he would have least dropped a hint. In spite of Berlitz's nervousness they were on very good terms, and Berlitz discussed nearly everything with him. This was a typical trick to undermine Pat's confidence in Berlitz. That's how Adolf ensures his safety, keeping everyone so suspicious that they never dare trust anyone enough to unite against him.

Adolf drew his eyes into sternness. "You are keeping bad company, you must choose your intimate friends better."

"But, Uncle," Pat began, "I don't."

"Yes," he repeated severely, "you are keeping bad company, dangerous company, and you had better choose better in the future. It is up to you to learn how to behave. Otherwise ..."

Almost without intention Pat parroted him. "Otherwise?"

It was too much. Adolf's fist resounded against the desk's heavy top. "You'll do as I say. Now you know what I expect, see that I get good reports of you in the future." He sat down heavily and drummed his fingers; yet a moment later, when he spoke again, his voice was quite calm, almost off-hand. "By the way, about your trip to England, I feel quite sure, when you think it over, you'll change your mind. I don't believe it would be desirable for you to go just now."

After a few more remarks the interview ended.

When Pat got back to the bank, Director Berlitz congratulated him. Schaub had telephoned that the Führer's instructions were that Pat's salary was to be doubled. Definitely Adolf didn't want Pat to go back to England. Next day Pat received his first and last present from the Führer, 100 Reichs-marks.

8

"Well, Mother," Pat continued, "you might have supposed I'd be satisfied now that I was getting twice as much money. But Uncle Adolf's words started me thinking. What did he mean when he said I was keeping bad company?"

Pat thought over all the people he knew. It was a long list because, as I mentioned before, he was invited everywhere. He always had his pick of three or four dinner parties on any given day, and often had to decline half a dozen weekend invitations.

"It was true I had met some pretty questionable characters." Pat told me that they were members of Adolf's intimate circle. "And anyway, you may be sure that I didn't go around with them. Take a man like Carl Ernst, for example. He used to be a waiter. He was a great friend of Uncle Adolf's and the head of the Berlin SA until 30 June – very tall, always well-groomed and too good-looking. When he was given Berlin as a present, it went to his head. He was crazy about cars, bought six (the most expensive kind) and never paid for them. He made the rounds of the cafés every night, always with young boys. One time I met him, he was with a boy nick-named 'Peppo', his friend, both drunk. Ernst kept fooling around with his gun, and finally shot a big wall mirror into a mass of splinters. Glass all over the place. But they didn't dare say a word. Ernst didn't leave until much later, and then only to keep Peppo from making up to a man named Vogel, who came in with another of Ernst's boyfriends. A former dress designer became Ernst's adjutant.

"Vogel was pretty awful too … one of those big fellows, all soft fat and three chins. He had a magnificent country place with a swimming pool, where he kept open-house for his 'boys'. Every guest-room was supplied with large bottles of the most expensive French perfume.

"Then there was the Reichs-sport-leader, von Tschammer und Osten. He was another of Adolf's functionaries who hung around the night spots, particularly the Custonlery Café. After one bottle of champagne he had to play the piano, no matter where he was or who was playing. If there was a piano he couldn't be stopped, until he fell off the stool senseless. And in summer he'd always take off his uniform coat and sit around in his braces. He spent most of his time with dancers, actresses, sports people and the lower kind of riff-raff.

"The licentiousness of Uncle Adolf's inner circle is well known; at weekend parties he's usually the only one to stay sober. Göring is a morphine addict, Röhm is a homosexual, Ley is a chronic alcoholic, but Adolf never objects to what they do on moral grounds. Instead he finds their carrying-on a good foil for his asceticism.

"It was impossible that Uncle Adolf was referring to that sort of thing. Although I knew, or had known, most of these people, they were his friends, not mine."

As Pat paused to light a cigarette, I thought of how dulled one's perceptions became to shocking things. When we in England had first heard about the goings-on of Adolf and his cronies, it had seemed pretty sickening, but then as one thing piled on another we began to take this sub-human society for granted. It had been necessary for me to hear these incidents from the mouth of my son to renew the shocked impression their nastiness had originally made on me. I suppose one always thinks of perverts, sex-maniacs and murderers as living in other places; it is almost inconceivable to think of them as being in daily association with your own family.

But Pat was speaking again.

"I thought of asking Director Berlitz what might have been meant, but hesitated after Uncle Adolf's remarks, even though I felt sure he had spoken with the intention of making me suspicious.

"At that time I had a room in the Lutzingerstrasse which I was sharing with cousin Leo, Aunt Angela's son. He knew everyone I did. I asked him which of my so innocent friends he though Adolf meant.

"'He means me,' Leo said. 'You're crazy not to have thought of it. Adolf has no scruples about the morals of his friends. No, it's not the Berlin night life, it's my company he's complaining about.'

"Thinking over it now," Pat continued, "I realise Leo was right. He was my 'bad company'. Uncle's hint, translated into plain English, meant, 'Keep away from Leo and his affairs'."

Leo's story, as Pat related it to me, was as follows:

It begins on 20 September 1931. Leo was in Linz, teaching school, when his mother – my sister-in-law, Angela Raubal – telephoned him from Munich that Geli had committed suicide. Completely shocked by this tragic news, Leo had no reason for doubting his mother's statement. Angela then told him that she was coming to Vienna with the coffin, and asked him to catch the train to Linz; they could then go on to Vienna together.

Leo, grieving for his beloved sister, went to the railroad station at Linz to meet his mother and help her fulfil her sad errand. As he waited for the Vienna train, the first doubt began to torment him. Why was his mother going to bury Geli in Vienna, when they had lived for years in Munich? Her adoring Uncle Adolf also lived in Munich. Then why transport her body across the border into Austria?

Still greater doubt assailed Leo's imagination when the burial ceremony, arranged by his mother, included full Catholic rights, an impossibility in the case of suicides, unless the Church judge the victim's mind was 'clouded'. Only one exception had been made: when Rudolf Habsburg killed himself, the Church granted special permission for his interment with full rites, but only after old Franz Joseph had begged for the privilege.

After the ceremony, Leo sought out Pater Paunt, who had officiated, and requested an explanation. The priest replied: "My poor friend, if your sister had committed suicide, I could not have performed the ceremony. You must be content with this. More I cannot tell you."

For Leo the solution of the minor puzzle was not difficult. Geli had not committed suicide, and his mother intended to keep it a secret. But the greater riddle remained. To clarify this mystery, Leo got leave of absence from his teaching job in Linz and went to Munich. The terrible suspicion that had seized on him was becoming an obsession. Knowing his mother would never speak, he must seek information elsewhere.

Living on the scant returns of tutoring, Leo pursued his quest, by accident encountering Dr Fritz Gerlich, ex-chief editor of the *Münchener Neueste Nachrichten*. Dr Gerlich, a fervent Catholic, had created a new weekly *Der Gerade Weg* (The Right Way) with only one aim, to combat Hitlerism, which he recognised as a deadly menace to the Catholic religion. The peculiar circumstances attendant on Geli's death suggested it might be a formidable weapon for attacking Hitler. Possibly Hitler's downfall might be ensured if it could be proved he had killed her. For months Dr Gerlich continued his investigation, embodying his results in a pamphlet, the title of which was inspired by Emile Zola's famous 'J'Accuse'. The evidence accumulated by Dr Gerlich's detective work pointed inevitably to one verdict – murder.

Geli had wanted to go to Vienna to make a career as a singer: A few days before her death she had been to a famous music critic, Willie Schmidt, and had asked him for letters of introduction to take with her. In Schmidt's affidavit given to Gerlich he states that Geli had given as one of her reasons for wishing to go there a desire to free herself from the molestations of her uncle.

Another affidavit is that of the police captain, who visited the Prinzregentenstrasse apartment and had questioned Josephine Bauer, the housekeeper. His judgement was that Adolf Hitler was in the apartment at the time the fatal shot was fired.

Although Adolf stated officially that he had left to go to Hamburg, Gerlich established that he had postponed his trip and remained all night in Munich. The proprietor of the Bratwurstglöckl Restaurant, Herr Senter, furnished an affidavit to the effect that Adolf had come to his restaurant with his niece and remained there until nearly one o'clock, occupying a private room on the first storey. In this statement was also noted that fact that Adolf was slightly intoxicated, as a result of drinking beer, an extremely unusual practice for him.

Gerlich, in the resumé of his pamphlet, reconstructed the 'crime'. According to him the rest of the night passed as follows:

After Adolf and Geli left the restaurant they returned to the apartment at about one o'clock. Happy to find himself alone with her, Adolf renewed his advances, which Geli opposed. During the discussion he threatened her with the service revolver he habitually wore. Certainly there was a struggle and during it a shot was fired.

One of the most interesting views of this pamphlet to my mind is that Gerlich gives no credence to the story told to Pat by Maimee that Geli was pregnant. Gerlich's opinion is that this version was invented by Hitler's accomplices with the object of providing the public with a credible motive for suicide. That Angela – Geli's mother – consented to spread this story is an interesting sideline on the hold Adolf has over her.

When Leo got hold of Gerlich's pamphlet he immediately made contact with him at Munich and learned many details he had not previously known.

Gerlich claimed that Göring undoubtedly did nearly as good a job in hushing up the affair as he had in the famous camouflage of the Reichstag fire. His stormtroopers successfully prevented any public clamour by stifling all press comments, and, of course, appropriate means were devised to silence witnesses.

Another friend of Hitler's denounced by Dr Gerlich was the Bavarian Minister of Justice, a seasoned party member, named Franz Gürtner, who helped force a definition of the mysterious death as suicide over the protestations of Glaser, the public prosecutor.

This assistance was the third to have been rendered to Adolf by Gürtner. When Adolf was sentenced to eight years in 1923, Gürtner had arranged for him to be released on 'parole' – an impossibility for anyone previously sentenced. Then too, according to German Law, Adolf, since he was Austrian not German, could have been deported, had not Gürtner helped him to remain.

The pamphlet shed a clear light on Adolf's decision to send Geli's body to Austria for burial. It was to avoid the exhumation which would inevitably follow the re-opening of the case. When Adolf became Chancellor, he brought Geli's body back to Germany. It now reposes in Berchtesgaden in a magnificent sarcophagus, which doesn't bear her name.

Dr Gerlich's pamphlet was placed in Hindenburg's hand a few weeks before the fateful 30 January, on which

Hitler was appointed Chancellor. But the course of the Nazi juggernaut was not to be stopped by one man's crime, 'murder'. A few days after Adolf's accession to power, Leo told Pat, Dr Gerlich was arrested, to be permanently silenced in the 30 June bloodbath, which unquestionably had for one of its objects the erasing from the record of the Führer's sins.

When Pat came to this point in telling me Leo's story, he was completely carried away by his emotions. Listening to his terrifying words, I began to realise the kind of thing we had got into. Trickery, tyranny and murder were words that had existed for me only remotely. To hear them brought to flesh-and-blood existence by my own son was a shattering experience. The complacency which had weakened the impact of the many shocking truths which I had learned at a comfortable distance, was dissolving with each word uttered by my son's firm English voice. What I might have thought exaggeration or imagination on the part of an excited foreigner, was doubly powerful on the lips of my reserved son. I had never heard him say so much before. Only an unparalleled urgency could account for it.

We had both stopped for breath, but now I was so eager to hear the rest that I urged him to go on.

After Gerlich's arrest, Leo went to Berlin. That was where Pat had met him, in Alois's restaurant, and offered to share his apartment with him.

At first Leo didn't trust Pat. In company with many others, he thought Pat was on good terms with Adolf, as he was the only heir to his name. But after Pat had confessed his troubles to Leo, and repeated his conversations with Geli, he took Pat into confidence. Through all of one night they spoke, and although they had been friends before, for the first time they came really to know each other.

Leo told Pat: "I could think of nothing except my poor sister Geli, and what Adolf did to her, and after I talked with Dr Gerlich I was more than ever convinced that I had to do something."

"And what do you think happened that night?" Pat asked Leo.

He said: "Look, my friend, I know very well what was going on at the Prinzregentenstrasse apartment. Geli was killed with a revolver. In that apartment there was only one, Adolf's. He has used it more than once as a threat against me too. I will tell you only one incident. I had been going around with a girl. Adolf was violently against our engagement, because she was the daughter of a carpenter and Adolf didn't want what he considered a misalliance in the family. He had ordered Mother to put an end to the affair. In order to pacify Adolf she told him it was all over. Unfortunately, however, the girl was pregnant and I felt I should marry her at once. In desperation I went to Berchtesgaden in Adolf's absence and tried to enlist Geli's aid. Adolf came in. When he found out what had happened he fell into such a rage that he yanked out his revolver and threatened to make an end of me. Geli intervened. I think it was the same scene which took place between Adolf and Geli. And don't forget that Senter said Adolf had been drinking beer. He wasn't himself. Even one glass was enough to make him tipsy.

"And what was her mother's attitude towards this affair?" Pat asked Leo.

"That's the most difficult question you could ask me," Leo told Pat. "I am sure my mother knows what happened. She was really Adolf's accomplice, because she tolerated his making love to Geli. She knew; yet she did nothing. Was she afraid? Possibly. Or was it only that she did not want to give up her comfortable life? When Geli was shot I suppose Mother felt it was useless to quarrel with Adolf over it. Geli was irrevocably lost to her: why should she lose Adolf too? It is difficult for a son to say it of his mother," Leo concluded steadily, "but I believe she should share Adolf's punishment as well as his guilt."

During the rest of Leo's stay with Pat, he steadfastly refused to have anything to do with Adolf. Angela did all she could to make him change his mind. But he was not to be moved. One day Schaub came to the flat, bringing a message, or rather an order, from Adolf for Leo to come and see him at once. Leo's reply was a flat statement: "I refuse to speak with the murderer of my sister."

Pat said it was quite a scene. Schaub turned and stared lengthily at Pat, as though to say, "You'll be sorry for this." But Leo was in such a white hot fury, there was no question of quietening him. Schaub left precipitately.

"But what do you mean to do"' Pat asked Leo several times. "You're fighting against a windmill. All the power is on Adolf's side. What can you hope to accomplish?"

Leo replied: "I am a fool, I know, even if I could kill Adolf, it wouldn't bring my sister back, but I can think of nothing else. My aim is to bring him before an independent court and accuse him of murdering her."

"If you think that's possible, you're crazy," Pat told him.

"Perhaps I am only one, but you are another against him. Tomorrow there may be five and in a year …?"

Pat, who had been recounting the story to me so

vividly that I felt almost as though I had been present myself, fell silent, his expression thoughtful.

"Then where is Leo now?" I asked him.

"I don't know what happened to him, Mother. One day he told me he was going back to Austria. He had heard that Schuschnigg had also made researches on the subject of Geli's death for his dossier on Adolf. I didn't hear anything more directly, but someone told me he was shot by the customs guard as he was about to cross into Austria. But he wasn't killed. They took him to a Salzburg hospital. A month later someone broke into his room and killed him. The Austrian authorities were unable to trace the murderer. Of course nobody will be in a position to state that it was done on Uncle Adolf's orders. You can't imagine, Mother, how things are done here unless you actually see. Brückner and Schaub are just like the slaves of some Oriental despot. If they got the idea that Uncle Adolf wanted Leo killed, they'd by quite likely to execute Adolf's orders even before they were given. Only one thing I'm sure of, Leo signed his own death warrant, when he openly stated that the Führer had murdered his sister."

9

For a long time there was a silence in the room. Pat came to his feet and walked up and down the room a few times. Then he came back to the window, looking nervously at me as though I should produce the key to this situation. "And now that you've heard all this, do you think I am seeing things too black? Or must I consider the possibility that I might come to a similar end one day? I was glad you were in London, for I don't believe that Adolf, Schaub or Himmler would risk doing anything to me so long as you could make a scandal in England. At first I couldn't credit the idea forming in my mind, it seemed too fantastic to believe, but after Leo died I could find no other explanation. It was then I began to wonder when my turn would come. The more I thought about it, the more convinced I became, that the only reason no 'accident' has happened to me is that they didn't have you here. I'm sure now that you saved me from the 30 June purge."

Although when we first began to speak I assured my son I could 'be a man', I felt my resolution swiftly ebbing away. "I don't understand, Pat. How could my not being here save you?"

"You'll understand soon enough," said Pat.

Since Pat's earlier contretemps with Adolf, which ended in an increase in salary, Director Berlitz at the bank had taken it for granted that Pat was on good terms with the Führer.

Like all friendships in Nazi Germany, theirs was constantly being menaced by suspicion and fear. But Pat felt that Berlitz was one of his few sincere friends. One reason for Pat's belief was that Berlitz, in spite of Pat's relationships with the Führer, confided in Pat in a way which was unusual in those hazardous days. He also frequently entertained him socially.

On 29 June 1934 – it was Friday afternoon – Director Berlitz invited Pat to accompany him on a weekend trip to Badpiermont near Hanover. On the way back they got the first report of Röhm's sensational arrest. Pat could see that Berlitz was getting panicky, and before they got to Berlin Berlitz told Pat why. Schulz, the 'political commissar' who had been put in the bank to watch out for the interests of the Nazis, might take this chance to get even with Berlitz for the run-ins they'd had, when Schulz gave particularly stupid or unfeasible orders. Like most of the little Spiessbürger who got themselves cushy jobs, he never missed an opportunity to demonstrate his authority over the men who would normally boss him. And he loved to shout at them in a blustering tone with threatening gestures; this was particularly incongruous because he had only one arm. Pat had never been able to understand why Berlitz had allowed him so much leeway, but then, as he said ruefully, he was very green and due to be educated. Once Berlitz's tongue had been unleashed, Pat began to understand many things that had previously puzzled him. It became clear that although Berlitz was the director of the bank, he was merely a front behind which the Nazis operated as they wished. It was well-known in banking circles that as soon as the Nazis came to power they began using depositors' money for their own use.

On Monday morning Pat and Berlitz returned to a terrorised Berlin. "Unless you have gone through it," Pat said, "you cannot imagine what it was like. In the still cool morning you could almost smell the panic that gripped the city. Little knots of men shrank tighter, or slipped into doorways as we passed them, fear betraying itself in their swiftly sidelong glances, the furtive coming-together of heads. Normal traffic had diminished, few pedestrians ventured on the street, there was a spurious calmness, as though the city were waiting, breath held in dread of what was still to come. At intervals the clangour of the uniform-filled trucks reverberated against the deadness of the atmosphere. Heavy tyres hummed along the pavement. Sirens shrieked."

And when they arrived at the bank, Director Berlitz began discreet inquiries. After an hour, he called Pat into his private office. What Berlitz said wound up the story Pat was attempting to squeeze from the melodramatic newspaper accounts of treason and punishment. Röhm, Hitler's staunchest supporter and commander of the S.A., had already been executed, along with Ernst and Heines, for participation in an alleged putsch.

"But it's my private opinion," Director Berlitz commented to Pat in a shaky voice, "that it was just the other way around: they were out to get Röhm and his men in the SA who might prove troublesome. General Schleicher and his wife were shot. Papen was arrested. God knows how many others. No one is immune. They even say Göbbels may have been knocked off by Göring."

A few hours later three SS men swaggered into the bank. Schulz, around whom everyone's suspicions and anxieties had been circling all morning, remained in his place. No one looked directly at the intruders; all waited to see where the blow would fall.

The SS men strode forward, their hands on their heavy service revolvers. When they came to Schulz they stopped and stared contemptuously at him. His faced turned as white as his collar. When one man let his hand fall on his shoulder the wretch began to whimper. Like a stubborn schoolboy he clung desperately to the edge of his desk with his hands, but it was useless. One of the SS men cracked him on the side of the head with his revolver butt, and Schulz went sliding down under his desk, limp as a fish. Clutching him by the collar, the SS

149

men jerked him off his chair and then pulled him towards the door, followed by his two comrades, who didn't even bother to pick up the unconscious man's legs, but let them drag along the floor.

At ten o'clock that evening, as every evening, Pat was sitting at a sidewalk table, in the Kransler Café, a popular place on the corner of Unter den Linden and Friedrichstrasse.

Berlin's heart was beating with a dulled rhythm, as though drugged with fatigue after the day's sensation. Few people had ventured forth to their usual haunts.

New rumours spread through the sparsely populated café, like the ripples of waves when a stone is dropped. Some came from radio loudspeakers, some were invented.

Every few minutes SS patrols passed. One of these, consisting of four men, led by a tall stormtrooper with a scar on his cheek, and a stocky fellow who had obviously had more than a few drinks, entered the café. The men officiously went around, demanding to see the papers of all the guests. As each table was cleared, they moved on to the next. Apparently they were looking for someone, rather than making a routine check. But they didn't stop over any of the papers for more than a casual glance until they came to Pat.

Pat had already taken out his wallet containing his working papers, a few letters and his visiting card, which were the only things he had with him.

The tall stormtrooper, staring at Pat's National Health card, which he held in his hand, spoke without looking up. "Your name."

Since Pat's name was printed on the card in sizable letters it was quite impossible that the stormtrooper could have failed to see it. Nevertheless Pat told him.

The response came, not from him, but from his shorter companion, who bellowed in a voice like a frog: "The Führer's name is not to be used for stupid jokes."

"What is your name?" the tall one repeated, emphasising each word as though his patience had been overstrained already.

Pat repeated it.

A third was mockingly polite. "I suppose you claim to be a relative of the Führer?"

When Pat said he was Adolf Hitler's nephew the tall one came closer. "That's a good joke. Now I'll tell one." Then in a changed voice he ripped out: "Get up. You're under arrest."

"But …"

"Shut your filthy mouth or I'll shut it for you," he roared.

Those were the formalities of Pat's arrest. The tall one seized him roughly by the shoulders, and shoved him into the street, where he nearly upset a passer-by. In a moment the street was empty.

At the kerb was a big Mercedes Benz.

Pat was thrust into the rear, sandwiched between the tall trooper and the stocky one, while two others got in front and two rode the running board.

During the short ride that followed, Frog-voice kept grumbling in a maudlin way at Pat's insolence at claiming relationship with the Führer. The ones who had piled into the front were silent except to laugh uproariously at Pat's drunken tormentor, when he complained, "Any lump-head might claim he's related to the Führer."

They drew up in front of the Reichswehr ministry. Inside Pat was placed under guard and left to his thoughts.

His first surprise was over. Now, as he waited for someone to come and rectify the error that had obviously been made, his temper began to rise. As time passed, Pat said, he could feel his patience stretching thinner and thinner until it was like a tensed rubber band.

When a young Reichswehr Lieutenant entered and began to question Pat in a roundabout routine way, he tried to be correct and formal. But each additional question was like pumping oil on a blazing fire. The Lieutenant seemed to be trying to hide behind a wall of red tape. Even when Pat told him his name, it was as though nothing had registered on his passivity. If he could only penetrate that blank façade, Pat thought. And then the Lieutenant asked him yet another question, which it seemed to Pat he had answered a dozen times already. Barely conscious of what he was doing, Pat swept the papers off his desk with one motion of his arm and pounded his fist on the table.

"It's a mistake, you idiot. Can't you understand? It's a mistake." The words rushed from Pat's lips. He found he was shouting at the Lieutenant – who he was, where he worked. He was offering references, including Director Berlitz and Alois.

The young Lieutenant was scarcely more surprised by Pat's outburst than he was. For a moment he stared at Pat, and at the mess he had made. Then, as though suddenly making up his mind, he muttered something like an excuse and left Pat alone. It wasn't until the door was closed behind him that Pat noticed he had smashed his ring when he had struck the table.

When the Lieutenant came back, a note bordering an apology was in his voice. "It's best for you to remain here for the present," he said, "until they calm down a bit." He made a despairing gesture with his hand, which seemed to indicate a multitude of unutterable regrets, as he continued: "You see, they can do anything they like. There is no authority over them except the highest."

Without another word he left Pat again, this time not to return for more than an hour. "There is nothing I can do," he said bitterly. Pat suddenly was aware that much more than his affair was at stake for the Lieutenant. "They insist on taking you with them. There is no way I can stop them. I'm sorry."

Roars of laughter were the signal that Pat's captors were back, all six of them and very much the worse for the drinks they had apparently been guzzling since Pat saw them last. Though jostled and man-handled, Pat wasn't really injured as they made their way back to the car, into which they all wedged themselves. As they started off with a lurch, the stormtroopers began to fling insults and threats about.

"Take a good look," warned the stocky one. "It'll be your last chance."

"How can you be so mean to him?" derided the third.

"Hope he's made his will."

"I knew it was useless to try to make a break for it," said Pat, describing his feeling at this moment. "They'd probably beat me to a jelly, as I knew had happened with countless others who'd ventured to oppose the SS boys. Were they taking me for a ride like the gangsters in the films? Were they really after me, or was it all an error? I was sure they had made a mistake, but if I antagonised them, or some whim started them mauling me, it wouldn't be much consolation to you, Mother, to received an apology for a 'regrettable accident', with my ashes. No, the only course I could pursue was to sit tight and try not to accelerate their sport. So long as they were content with insulting me I was all right."

The car jolted to a stop at Lichterfeld, a kind of concentration camp on the outskirts of the city. One glimpse of the hive humming with uniformed men made Pat wonder if he was better, or worse off, now that he had reached his destination. The eager guards rushed Pat before the officer in charge, who promptly ordered him to a cell pending investigation. He had no opportunity to do more than glance right and left as the new guard hustled him away, but what he saw was hardly reassuring. Machine guns were blatantly in view; uniformed men were everywhere; new 'criminals' were already being brought in as Pat was taken out. The scene was distinctly sobering.

Pat was put in a cell with two men in SA uniforms, whose insignia indicated high rank. One of them, glancing suspiciously at Pat, demanded, "Who are you?" Once more his truthful response elicited a startled guffaw. "At least," his questioner consented, "we're hearing a good joke before they finish us."

And that was the end of the conversation. Each of them sat muffled in his troubles, until an hour later, when Pat's questioner was sent for.

"Where to?" he asked the SS man who had come for him.

"You know well enough," was the laconic reply.

Pat's remaining cell-mate shook hands with the one who was being taken away. "Adolf Hitler has betrayed us," he said in a low voice.

The condemned man squared his shoulders, and shook his head. "No, my friend," he said, "the Führer knows nothing of this. I am sure of that. If he knew ..." His right hand shot into the air and his voice resounded hollowly: "Heil Hitler!"

At four in the morning they sent for Pat. He repeated his story. The officer in charge almost duplicated the attitude of the one in the Reichswehr office. "I have no control over the men who arrested you. There is nothing I can do."

"The police commissioner von Levetzow knows me," Pat suggested. "Call him up. He'll be able to identify me."

"We can't awaken the Police Commissioner at this hour," was the officer's toneless response.

Pat knew that wasn't true. The flatness of the officer's voice left no loophole for persuasion. Pat tried a new tack. "What's going to be done with me?" he demanded.

"That's up to the men who arrested you," the officer replied.

There must be some way out of this mess; he had to do something. Well, why not go to the top, then? Why not seek his uncle's help? He had nothing to lose.

"Please call the Chancellery," Pat was saying in an authoritative tone. "Rudolf Hess, or my uncle, will confirm my identity – or his adjutants, Schaub and Brückner. They know me."

The officer's expression was a curious puzzle of emotions as he stared fixedly at Pat. Was he annoyed? Certainly it wasn't antagonism on his face. Almost, Pat thought, he was sorry. It was only after an embarrassingly long pause that he said quietly: "All right, I'll see."

Although Pat hadn't seen Adolf for some time, he had every confidence that Adolf would help him. His arrest had been a terrible mistake.

Ten minutes later the adjutant's officer returned. "I

155

spoke to Schaub," he reported.

Pat waited for him to continue.

"Schaub says the Führer has no nephew."

As Pat paused after repeating Schaub's brutal words, I suddenly felt a heavy pounding in my heart, against my ribs. It was just as though I too had been in that cell with him and had heard those brutal words, "The Führer has no nephew."

"But what happened? How did you escape?" I could hardly wait for him to catch his breath.

"Partly luck and the rest a question," Pat replied. "You see, Uncle Adolf was establishing a new order in Germany, but there are fortunately still quite a few loose ends. And it was one of these that led me out of my labyrinth."

When the guard who was to see Pat back to his cell took him to the main part of the building, they found themselves in a regular pell-mell. Hundreds of prisoners had been brought in. Hundreds of others were being herded about, transferred, or led to execution. So many of them were in uniform that it was unbelievably confusing, and this turned out to Pat's advantage, because the bewildered guard took him to another cell, in a different part of the building. Consequently Pat's kidnappers must have fallen into a stupor long before they could track him down, and an hour later he was given a hearing before another officer, who had no idea who he was, or that this was a special case. Realising that the mistake gave him the one chance in a thousand he hadn't dare hope for, Pat replied to the first question in English. "My name is William Patrick," he said. "I am a British subject."

When the officer spoke again in German, Pat replied in that language, but with an atrocious accent. "Please allow me to call the British consulate. A mistake has been made."

The officer agreed to telephone, and Pat was permitted to remain in the office. During the hour that ensued, he had plenty of time to take stock of the situation. Had Pat's drunken abductors happened on him fortuitously, or was it planned with the full approval of the higher-ups – even perhaps the Führer himself? Had Schaub acted on his own authority in denying Pat, or under orders?

Towards six in the morning, an attaché of the British consulate arrived. Fortunately he had met Pat several times and recognised him at once, but he said nothing about the changed name.

"I don't know that I have ever been so glad to see a fellow-countryman," Pat commented.

As soon as the officer saw that the attaché recognised Pat, they both went out. Ten minutes later, Pat was released.

"I was free," said Pat. "But even now I don't know exactly how. The Gestapo is very efficient. I am sure I was on a list. Otherwise I wouldn't have been arrested, particularly in a café where I was known to go every evening. And then, when the tall trooper with the scar made fun of my name, I was sure that he knew quite well all the time who I was, or he wouldn't have dared to take a chance testing me. Yes, certainly I was on the list. Schaub's telephone repudiation made that clear. Yet they changed their minds in the Chancellery. Certainly that was because of you. If the man who had arrested me had finished me off immediately it might have been a regrettable accident, but to dispose of me later was too risky, particularly as you were in England and not likely to take lying down anything that might happen to me."

"If I had only known," I found myself repeating.

"Good God, if I had only known. But isn't there any way to get back to London. Couldn't the man from the consulate help us?"

Although Pat's next words were anything but comforting, his grasp of the situation reassured me a little. "To attempt to go back to London would be the worst possible move on our part. I have had my British passport the whole time I've been here, so officially I would have been able to leave at any time, but I realised almost from the beginning that to leave openly would be taking my life in my hands. By the time the British authorities could do anything it might be too late, and of course you are officially an Austrian. The only thing we can do, Mother, is to continue the policy I've been following up to now. Pretend you're satisfied and keep smiling. Don't let them see for a moment you have the slightest suspicion that everything isn't as it should be. Agree to everything and, no matter who speaks to you or how plausible they sound, never forget that whatever you do will be recorded and the least thing you say or do used against you."

"But what will be the end of it? How long are we going to have to put up with it? Is there any chance of our getting out of here?'

The practical determination with which I spoke must have appealed to my son's sense of humour, for he suddenly smiled – as he does sometimes, and then the whole atmosphere changes, and he looks very young and extremely handsome. As a matter of fact, it was rather funny to think of us, two ordinary citizens conspiring like thieves in a den against a man who had grown before our very eyes into the most ruthless warlord of them all. If we got out of this it would be due only to our Irish stock. We both laughed and hugged each other, once more in possession of ourselves. We weren't going to give up without a fight. We began to make our plans. "We have one chance, Mother. It all depends on who's the better chess player, Adolf or I." Pat laughed mischievously. "I don't mean real chess, of course. I'm pretty sure Adolf doesn't play that. I've worked out a plan that should spring this trap, but the first step is to get you out of this accursed country."

"Me … but what about you?"

"Don't you understand, Mother? Once you're outside the country I'll be much safer, but you have to go first. And you must do it in such a way that no one suspects your reason for leaving."

Pat had based his plan of escape upon Adolf's sister Paula, who was living in Vienna. When Adolf Hitler's notoriety was growing and it became known to him that his two sisters had become the centre of public interest in the Austrian capital, he proposed that they should move to Munich. His invitation was gratefully accepted by the widowed Angela who, having three children, found it very convenient to live under the protection of her brother, particularly since it included their support.

Paula, unlike her sister, didn't accept Adolf's invitation. In fact she didn't even acknowledge it directly. Alois had received a letter from her, which Maimee showed to Pat on one of his first visits to Germany. In it Paula gave her reason for not wishing to take up with him. Adolf, she said, though her real brother, had left her on her own when she was only ten years old (she and Adolf had come to Vienna to stay with their older sister Angela after their mother died). Adolf, Paula continued, went to the war and she didn't hear from him again. At the end of the war he was only a few hours away from where she still lived, but he never bothered to send her so much as a postcard, until he found it annoying to have two poor sisters in Vienna. Then he invited them both to come to Munich. Adolf didn't mind, Paula complained, that she had to live for years on Aunt Angela's charity. Nor did he care that she never married, always waiting for the day when Adolf would come back. "I never want to see him again" was Paula's conclusion.

Although not particularly intelligent or well-trained, Paula had managed to support herself by doing office work. When Adolf had learned that she was a typist in the employ of a Jewish insurance man, he begged her at least to give up this embarrassing association, even if she would not come to Munich as he wanted. Angela, always the go-between in family matters, carried back the message that time that Paula was not interested in Adolf's anti-Semitism, which she found ridiculous, and that she had no intention of giving up her job. Since Adolf was not supporting her, she added, she could think of no reason he should be concerned. Adolf's reaction was to offer her 100 Schillings a month (about $20, £4) if she would change her mind. Eager as he was to force her agreement, he couldn't miss mentioning that this meagre support would be sent to her in three instalments, so that she would not be tempted to spend it all at once! This infuriated Paula. Her next indirect message to the Führer was a declaration that she wanted nothing to do with him, then or ever.

Years had elapsed since Angela had moved to Munich. During that time Adolf had tried every available means to conciliate Paula, who was his only real sister. Paula, however, stubbornly refused to answer any other letter or messages, regarding all approaches with the same contemptuous indifference. She continued to live in the same old attic apartment on Schönburgstrasse, under the name of Frau Wolf. When Adolf, through Angela, again and again offered financial aid to enable her to adopt the standard of living more nearly commensurate with his position in the world, she disdained it, saying she would never accept anything from him. The bitter letters she wrote to Angela never contained a single word of praise or appreciation of her brother. And after the death of Geli, she broke with Angela also.

My son intuitively sensed that Paula was the only person who might exert an influence on Adolf. Because he (Adolf) needed something from her, consequently she was the only member of the family who might be in a position to help him (Pat) escape. He wrote to her, she replied at length, and a correspondence began. From one of her letters Pat learned that she was experiencing difficulty living on the dole she received from some workers' compensation fund and was ill most of the time. Pat arranged for her to receive a small sum monthly, which Adolf provided. Paula was willing to accept it because she thought it came from Pat. Both Paula and Adolf were pleased.

This was the game of chess my boy was playing with his uncle. Pat felt sure that Adolf would do anything to get Paula into Germany, even have her kidnapped and brought there by force, though only for the satisfaction of making her do as he wanted. He was frustrated by Chancellor Schuschnigg of Austria, who provided a guard to watch over her to save her from constant molestations by German agents under Adolf's orders. As Paula was an Austrian she had a citizen's right to be protected against foreign agents. Since Pat was the only member of the family who had established a cordial relationship with her, it was reasonable to assume that, if Pat should undertake to reconcile her with Adolf, Adolf might accept his mediation and permit him to go to Vienna. Once there, Austria being a foreign country, the trap would have been sprung.

Now that I had arrived so inopportunely, Pat was obliged to alter his original scheme accordingly, shifting me into the role of the angel of reconciliation. I was to be the one to persuade Paula to leave Vienna and to come and live in Germany with her brother and half-sister.

"There's no point in my saying it's going to be easy, Mother," Pat warned me. "Not because of Paula ... she will be for us ... but Angela. She is the least understandable woman I ever encountered in my life. Though she has lost two of her children, under the most suspicious circumstances, she clings to Adolf with inexplicable stubbornness. Sometimes I feel as though she was his evil spirit, but it's probably the other way around." The day after I arrived we took a walk through Berlin seeing the sights. At noon we returned by way of the Unter den Linden and found a message that Angela was coming to visit me.

In mid-afternoon she arrived, a tall rather heavy woman with a kindly expression. She looked the part I knew she played, that of cook and housekeeper for her famous brother.

After we had chatted a while, Angela turned to Pat. I knew she meant it as a great compliment to me when she complacently informed me, "Willie looks exactly like Adolf, when he was his age, even more than like his father."

I acknowledged her politeness with as much grace as I could muster, and watched as she unfastened her voluminous handbag, and withdrew a pillow-cover, hand-embroidered with a swastika, which she ceremoniously presented to Pat, and a box of soap, even then a great luxury, which failed to nudge him.

After appropriate remarks had been made by all, Angela came swiftly to the real occasion of her visit, an expression of Adolf's wish to meet me.

"The invitation is for next Sunday week," Angela said in a curiously expressionless voice. "Naturally Willie is to accompany you."

Following my son's directions I expressed delight, and began saying the usual meaningless things. Angela's indifference toward the amenities, when she rather uncivilly interrupted me, clearly pointed to the second object of her sisterly visit.

"Have you had any news from Paula?"

This question, cutting incisively into the conversation, served to convince me that Pat's plan was based on an accurate grasp of family politics. And though this diplomatic manoeuvring smacked of the kind of pettiness I had all my life deplored, I realised the desperate situation in which we found ourselves the unwilling protagonists.

Yes, Paula was the weakest link in a chain which kept Adolf's personal history intact against the prying of international gossip-mongers. While she existed as a separate entity he could only insecurely fasten the glamorous mantle of an immaculate godhead around his shoulders. The fabric he had loomed with such elaborate care might appear as fustian after all, if seen too close.

These were the thoughts that were seething in my mind after Pat, having discreetly excused himself, read Paula's latest letter aloud to Angela, withdrawing to the window at which he had sat so long the day before. He was obliged to read it a second time, while Angela listened without interruption. At the conclusion Angela began to speak. She had been informed that Paula was considering writing her memoirs, and that she had already been conferring with an agency with that end in view.

If such a book were published, Angela concluded grimly, it would be a scandal. "But it is impossible. Adolf would never allow it."

After Angela left, Pat wrote to Paula announcing my desire to visit her. At the end of his letter I added a few lines to introduce myself.

For the evening also I had a rendezvous with my ex-husband. After Adolf became a power in Germany, Alois had given up his razor company to take over a luxurious restaurant not far from the Chancellery. Since many of the higher-up Nazis became frequenters, it proved considerably more profitable than the razor-blade business.

When Alois called and suggested he came to see me at Pat's hotel, where I had taken an adjoining room on the same floor, I refused. Though I harboured no ill-feeling against him for all the unhappiness he had caused me, I would have preferred to keep it all in the past. But Pat felt I should see him, if only to strengthen the impression we needed to create that I was planning to come to Germany for good. So when Alois proposed that as an alternative I go to see him at his restaurant I accepted, on condition that I wouldn't have to see Maimee. This was much better than having him come to the hotel, because at a public place there would be no opportunity for any intimate talk, and I made Pat promise that he would get other people to join the party.

On our way to the restaurant, at 3 Wittenbergplatz, I

asked Pat, "What about your father? How does he stand in this affair?"

"My father?" Pat smiled wrily. "He's so afraid, he'd even be capable of informing on me, if he thought that would get him into Adolf's good graces."

Perhaps my distress at the thought of meeting Alois again will seem silly, but it is difficult to renew the acquaintance of someone with whom you have once been in love. They say one returns always to one's first love – this was certainly not the case with me.

Alois's first words when we met proved to me he had not changed at all. Leading us towards the 'gala' table which he had specifically reserved for us, he drew me out of Pat's hearing. "Cece, darling," he began, "you know very well you were and are the only great love of my life, and if fate hadn't played such a cruel trick on us, we'd still be living happily together."

It was his old voice, old manner and old self all over again. Whenever he wanted something from me he would always tell me how much he loved me. I wondered what it was now.

Alois had succeeded in producing a first-class European restaurant, complete with bustling expert waiters, a faint odour of hot rolls and liquor, smooth white tablecloths with yellow borders, sparkling glasses and much loud talk and laughter.

As soon as we sat down I began to make polite conversation. Pat helped me avoid Alois by pointing out the important Nazis who were habitués of this sleek restaurant. There was Lützow, who had replaced Röhm in the SA In one corner was Leni Riefenstahl, the film director. All heads turned to stare when Göbbels came in with his attractive wife, both bowing like film stars.

Although it was still early, every corner was crowded. Most of the men wore dashing uniforms, many of the women Paris gowns. There were many theatrical people, even a few English ones, though no one I knew. The whole effect was gay and carefree, an extraordinary contrast to the eating places Pat and I had previously visited, where everyone looked threadbare and pinched. The food, too, was altogether of a different quality, richer and in great quantity.

I sipped my wine and looked about. Naturally I couldn't evade Alois entirely. He had taken the chair next to mine and began at once to speak of our happy life together.

Even on the first evening I was tired of the deception I had to practise. Certainly my temperament would not have been suited to a life of crime. Dissembling my real feeling for the benefit of my husband, the waiter who served us and a portly German who sat at our table (I learned later that he was von Dirksen, the ambassador to London) was one of the most exhausting things I ever tried to do. To consider every word before I uttered it, to control every gesture and facial expression, even under those not particularly wary eyes! I had never realised before what it was to be independent. I glanced at my son, who was nonchalantly engaged in conversation with a guest whose name I didn't recall. How could he appear so relaxed and diverted? Only a slight tightness of the mouth, a faint tenseness of his body portrayed his uneasiness to me. Remembering the candid impulsive boy I knew, I marvelled at his self-control – but then he'd been learning diplomacy in a hard school.

I turned to my husband, determined to emulate Pat's aplomb. "How does it happen, Alois, that your brother, who everyone tells me is a strict teetotaller, allows you to maintain such a lavish wine restaurant?"

Another note I knew, the sort of defiant peevishness a husband uses towards a wife when a question is often discussed but never settled, crept into Alois's voice. "This is my trade. Should I throw out money like water? I have always stood on my own two feet. I don't need Adolf's help. And anyway, what could he do for me? Make me a leader in his party? Zum Teufel, he has become a signpost to the whole German nation. He would never do anything that would give people cause to think he is supporting his family at the expense of the nation."

I wondered whom he was trying to convince, himself or me. Since he was so ready to talk, I determined to probe the subject a little more deeply.

"That's entirely understandable," I soothed him, "but since he makes such a point of economy and abstinence I wonder that he allows all this." My hand indicated the crowded restaurant, where some of the highest functionaries pointed out to me a few minutes before were making merry in a manner so lavish it would have put Monte Carlo to shame.

Alois's response was instantaneous. "Oh, Adolf himself enjoys a good time. That is a matter of his private life. And on that subject he permits no criticism." His tone lowered to a confidential murmur. "You know, Cece, there isn't one man in the Party who would dare say a word to Adolf about his private affairs, even before he became Chancellor. That was the one thing he wouldn't have. Gregor Strasser did go for him once, as spokesman for leaders of the Party, to complain that he was being seen too much with Geli, and that the Party administration feared that the opposition might use it as propaganda. What a temper Adolf flew into! 'What leader?' He thundered.

'What Party administration? I am the Party. I am the administration. I am prepared to lay my life down for this Party I created, created when it had seven Marks to its credit, and not even a rubber stamp. Go back, Strasser, and tell the men who have dared to send you on this errand and who lead only because I have so willed it, that I am the leader here, and if they do not like it they can get out.' Of course he was angry because they wanted him to turn over the Party's funds to it, but what infuriated him most was that they should think they had anything to say about his life, which 'concerned no one on this earth'. Ever since then to mention anything to do with his family has been strictly taboo. And that remind me of something else." Alois lowered his voice even more, so that no one seemed to be listening to us.

"When you see Adolf at Berchtesgaden, for heaven's sake be careful what you say. Take this as it's meant, the advice of a man to whom you are the dearest in the world. And whatever you do don't mention, or even hint at, the time you benefited us in Liverpool. After all, it was twenty years ago, it's perfectly reasonable to assume you might have forgotten. I hope you have really forgotten it, and anything I might have said in anger. How long do you plan to stay? I hope for a good long visit?"

I remembered my son's instruction about replying. "Visit, no, Alois. I'm thinking of coming here to live."

"That's wonderful," exclaimed Alois. Pat turned to me, a look of admiration on his face.

Next morning I was astonished to receive a visit from Rudolf Hess's adjutant. In his immaculate uniform exuding a faint odour of perfume, he looked exactly like a figure from an operetta. Clicking his heels, he very courteously addressed me in excellent English. Herr Hess was sorry, he informed me, that he did not come to call on me, but he hoped that I would find it convenient to visit him in his office at eleven.

The moment the elegant young officer had left, I hurried to Pat's room and told him what had happened.

"This is very important," Pat told me. "Hess is Adolf's right-hand man. Schaub and Brückner are close to him, but as bodyguards. Hess is really the only one who knows everything."

Among Hess's duties had been the supervision of Pat's career in the Reich after Adolf had decided to re-acknowledge that he had a British nephew. Warning Pat, on the penalty of his greatest displeasure, to avoid any discussion of family matters or relationship to himself, Adolf had turned Pat over to Hess, who had been made Reichsminister, and head of the National Socialist Party, a few weeks before. Hess was very kind to Pat in his stiff way. One of his first friendly offices was to introduce him to everyone he thought he should know, including Herr Stender, the head of the Verbindungsstab, which was a kind of link between the Party and the Government, the ill-fated Count von Spreti, and Chief of Staff Röhm, who at that time was at the height of his power. Pat commented that Hess had been ill at ease in Röhm's ornate offices, which were in great contrast to Hess's, even though both were in the same building. Another functionary Pat met through Hess was Gauleiter Bohle, the Head of the Deutschen-im-Ausland (Germans living abroad), who had gone to school with Hess and had also lived in England.

Hess usually conversed with Pat in English, which he called the second language, having learned it in Egypt where he was born, the son of a German importer.

After all I had heard about Rudolf Hess, I need hardly

say that it was with great curiosity that I looked forward to meeting the Führer's 'confidential personal secretary'. For that was what, in reality, Hess was. Since his devotion to the Führer was beyond question, it was naturally on his broad and willing shoulders that most of the nagging details and difficult commissions fell. He was not a power in Germany in the sense Röhm had been, or Göring and Göbbels continued to be; rather he was a combined watchdog and batman – if I may use so British an expression to convey of the German function. To be the Führer's intimate servitor must have satisfied some profound need of his fanatic nature, and during all the years of Adolf's vertiginous career, Hess alone retained his master's unfaltering trust.

Hess was ready to receive us as soon as we arrived, to keep our appointment in the Verbindungsstab on Wilhelmstrasse, the building which had once housed the bureau of President Hindenburg. A young adjutant in SS uniform ushered us into his office and then left after stamping out a brisk "Heil Hitler!"

There is not much point in describing the man whose appearance is now nearly as familiar as that of our most famous film stars. But the impact of his rather unusual personality is still so vivid that it is perhaps worth an attempt to convey it. Of all the people I met in Germany, he is the one I remember best, even though I met him for such a brief moment that it seems absurd that he should have impressed me so strongly. Perhaps it was the ice-cold determination I felt burning in him like a flame; perhaps it was only the oddly hypnotic stare of his light-coloured eyes, under those caricature black eyebrows. But when I tried to analyse my reaction, I felt sure it was something else. A man carries about with him the indefinable stamp of his innermost nature, which anyone with an eye can see. In Hess it was, at least for me, an absolute fixity of purpose, which formed the opaque centre about which his other traits more transparently revolved.

Our interview took place in Hess's thoroughly businesslike office, which was furnished with a large desk, lightwood files on either side of the room and a minimum of luxury. He spoke meticulous English, and was very polite, even offering Pat a cigarette, though he did not smoke himself.

Rudolf Hess's attitude was exactly that of a master of ceremonies at a royal court. He thanked me for coming. "It was my duty to come to you on my Führer's mission, but pressing business here made that awkward. Madame Raubal has already conveyed to you his invitation to visit him in Berchtesgaden, I believe. I should like to discuss with you another subject. I understand you have expressed a wish to remain here for good. That is most interesting news." Leaning forward, he picked up a file and glanced inside.

I thought a moment. I had told no one but Alois about my intentions. How was it possible that the words I had spoken to Alois at the restaurant were already known in the Reichskanzler? My God, what a situation!

But Hess was going on: "I have a few questions to ask you and a list of items that should be attended to in London and in Germany."

After I had replied to his routine questions, he looked at me with great seriousness. Then he launched himself into an account of how he had come to join Hitler's movement.

He had been a lieutenant in the German air force during the world war and had never really laid down his arms. At the end of the war he had viewed the power of the occupation of Germany like contingents of French-Moorish troops, convinced that the situation, which then existed, could not and must not go on. He dreamed of a leader who would save Germany. At twenty-two, he had written an essay, which he showed us, describing the qualifications of Germany's needed Saviour. When Hess, in 1921, first heard Hitler's speech in the Sternecker beer-hall in Munich he was convinced that "this was the man". Hess displayed to us scars on his neck and hands which he proudly claimed had come from brawls in which he had protected Adolf from physical injury.

"It is a great privilege to be a German citizen, madam. I think that must be your intention, if you are electing to remain here. In your case it is particularly appropriate since you are, in addition to being the Führer's sister-in-law, an Austrian citizen by marriage."

I felt Hess was a sincere, poised, disciplined man. Tall, powerful, soldierly, correct, polite and seemingly logical, he in every sense represents for me the best type Nazism could produce. And it is because of his sincere loyalty to a pathologically unsound cause, that he, more than any of the others, who are mere riff-raff, frightens me for the future of Germany. What has caused this cultivated man to join the Nazi rabble? If there are many like him – and although I did not meet them I know there must be – I know too that only death could unbalance their absolutely sure, though absolutely wrong, convictions.

I have not met many fanatics in my life, but it would have been impossible not to recognise that Hess was one of them. What causes a man like that to attach himself to a master like Adolf? It can be nothing but a blind, and in this case misplaced, faith.

Perhaps the strong strain of mysticism in Hess is the

explanation. He told us he had been greatly influenced by his early life in Alexandria. He is something of an occultist, and claims to have had remarkable experiences. He is also an ardent believer in astrology. According to his judgment, Hanussen, the Hungarian seer who was liquidated by Count Hellsdorf in the Grünewald, much to Hess's annoyance, was the greatest of the 'prophets' in Adolf's orbit.

As we were about to leave, Hess smiled courteously at Pat. "My friend," he said, "I should like to take this occasion to say to you, unofficially of course, that you would be doing a service to our Führer should you decide to take the same step your mother is contemplating and change your nationality." He laughed confidentially. "You must surely realise that it's a little embarrassing for the Führer to have English relatives."

At the conclusion of our talk, Hess accompanied us to the outer door. As we progressed towards it, there was a great deal of snappy saluting and Heil-Hitlering. How could so sinister a discipline have such an affable flavour? It was impossible not to laugh; yet no one knew better than I what deadly seriousness lay beneath the comic exterior.

10

Two days before we were due to leave, we received a reply to the letter we had written to Paula the day I arrived. After skimming the contents, Pat looked eagerly at me.

"Mother," he exclaimed, handing me the letter, "it's more than I dared hope for. Read what Paula says."

As I looked at Paula's letter, I found myself scrutinising it with heightened awareness, trying to find a clue to the bewildering behaviour of at least one of my inexplicable in-laws. It was neatly written and well spaced, surrounded by narrow but precise margins. Everything about it suggested the description my son had given me. The writer must be meticulous, determined, self-controlled and self-willed. She said she was going to Salzburg the following week, but could combine her trip with meeting me.

"She couldn't have picked a better time," Pat commented, "for you can see the mountains around Salzburg from Berchtesgaden. It's only a short drive."

"If we get permission for the trip," I said sceptically.

"No question about that," Pat cut in. "Adolf would already have received a copy of this letter from the censor, and will certainly give you permission to go."

"What about you?" I asked. "It seems to me that the time has come to make our plans for the future. What's going to happen to you, if I succeed in getting away? Don't you think Adolf will take it out on you?"

"Not if there's a perfectly reasonable excuse for your failure to return. That's what we have to find now. We've got to concoct something to explain why you don't come back. Suppose Paula should want to keep you with her. In that case my position here would even improve."

My journey to Berchtesgaden began with a disappointment. I was expecting Pat to drive me to Bavaria. I thought the two of us would be alone for hours, and we would be able to speak our minds without fear of eavesdroppers. Disappointed of this hope by Angela's decision to join us, we set off from Berlin, not by car, as planned, but by train, as Angela preferred that method of travel. It was about six o'clock when we reached Munich station. Baldur von Schirach, the head of the Hitler youth, his manner suggesting that he was the ambassador of a king, met us and rather pompously informed us that Adolf had sent his car to take us to Berchtesgaden.

As we sped through the Munich traffic everyone turned to stare, not at us, as I fleetingly thought, but at the well-known black Mercedes Benz, to catch a glimpse of the Führer.

Angela turned to me in a complacent way. "Would you like to see where the Führer lives in Munich?"

On my courteously murmured assent, she ordered: "Take us to the Führer's home."

No doubt she meant it kindly enough, but the odour of sanctity which wavered between us in the air, at the mention of the Führer, indicated all too clearly the situation in this country. I could understand the feeling of odd respect a foreigner in a remote corner of the Reich might feel for the dictator of Germany, but that Adolf's sister should refer to him in such pleasurably servile tones was a bit thick.

Fortunately the brevity of the ride prevented too long a contemplation of my reaction to Adolf-worship. We were already stopping at 16 Prinzregentenstrasse, an unpretentious building on the outskirts of the city.

Inside the front door we mounted a broad wooden staircase to the second storey. Through a door distinguished in no way from all the others, we entered the private flat of the German Chancellor.

Angela's bearing, while completely dignified, nevertheless exuded a certain pride as she ushered me through her domain. Can a living man haunt a dwelling place? Adolf, whom I knew now only as a stranger, had

175

somehow encrusted his personality there so strongly that I could almost feel his presence in that commonplace, though large, flat. Here he had relaxed and paid court to his niece, the blue-eyed and golden-haired Geli.

Angela's face was impassive as we stopped at the locked door she quietly informed me was her daughter's. Reaching into her pocket, like a châtelaine, Angela drew out a key and opened the door.

The first thing that struck my eye was a large portrait of Geli. Radiant beneath her halo of golden hair, she looked out upon the world with kindly merry blue eyes, plump, gentle and maidenly. She was the perfect symbol of the German Mädchen Adolf holds up as an ideal to the nation.

"Isn't she beautiful?" said Angela, remarking on my interest. "Herr Ziegler, the famous Munich artist, painted her. Adolf was so touched that he made Herr Ziegler a professor of the Bavarian Academy of Arts, by a special decree written out in his own handwriting." I glanced round the room, which had become an almost impersonal sanctuary.

"It was in this room that Geli died," Angela continued. She indicated a large gilded birdcage which hung near one of the windows. "Four canaries she used to have, given to her by Adolf. My God, how they used to sing!" Angela's eyes were moist with unshed tears as she spoke, but what dark thoughts moved inside her I couldn't fathom. "Everything is just as it was the day she died. Adolf will allow nothing to be changed. It was a great sorrow to him. Sometimes he comes here and stays for hours, mourning for her."

A shiver passed over me. How quiet the room must seem to Adolf now that the canaries had ceased their singing.

A slight movement at my side made me turn to Angela. Suddenly, without the slightest warning, her pale blue eyes overflowed with tears, which ran slowly down her cheeks.

She began to speak. "Yesterday I was walking down Potsdamerstrasse. In a shop window there was a beautiful birdcage. I started to go in the store to see how much it cost, and then I remembered, my poor little Geli is dead." Angela covered her face with her hands, and wept helplessly.

My mood remained sombre for hours after we had left Munich far behind us. Pat and Angela too were silent, whether buried in their own thoughts or tired from travelling I couldn't tell. It was not until I saw the Alpine peaks ahead of us catch fire from the setting sun that I realised we were drawing near our destination.

Rousing from my lethargy, I began asking questions about my surroundings. Angela, who was more than willing to play mentor, showered me with a wealth of information concerning both past and present.

Twenty-five years ago the village of Berchtesgaden slumbered snugly behind God's back. Approachable only by rugged mountain paths and an unimportant railroad line, it lured occasional tourists to its magnificent view of the Bavarian Alps.

If you were seeking a quiet vacation you might have taken one of the four guest rooms let to visitors by Bruno Buchner, a retired German colonial officer and his wife. Their house, in addition to its desirable location on top of the Obersalzberg, had a special appeal to the romantic. Judith Platter, the heroine of the famous German novel *Zwei Menschen* (Two People), had lived in it and a verifiable description of Platterhof, as the mountain house was named, could be read in German by any literarily inclined guest.

Early in the 1920s a friend of Buchner named Webber, a member of the Munich civil council, arrived at the Platterhof with a companion whom he introduced as Dr Wolf.

'Dr Wolf', self-described as a writer, rented one of the guest rooms and liked it well enough to occupy it almost uninterruptedly for a year. By that time he had become so enamoured of this idyllic mountain retreat that he determined to take up permanent residence and for this purpose bought and furnished a nearby house, Wachenfeld, when its owners moved away.

It was not until 1923, when the Munich putsch thrust its crooked finger into the news that Buchner penetrated the incognito of his quiet guest and the new owner of Wachenfeld. 'Dr Wolf' was Adolf Hitler.

After Adolf was released from Landsberg prison and recommenced his activities, the Berchtesgaden gossips had plenty to clack their tongues about. Why should a budding political leader conceal his identity and withdraw from the energising light of publicity into this outpost, from which commuting to Berlin was inconvenient and time-consuming?

During the gestation period of the Nazi movement, Adolf took every precaution to prevent its being aborted by the authorities, who took a keen, but by no means friendly, interest in its development. Foremost in his mind in observing these precautions was the protection of his own person. Obscurity was the ruse by which he sought to avoid their clutches, at the same time mysteriously contributing to the mystery already attached to his origin and private life.

Adolf insisted that nothing should be known about him but his name, for if nothing was known anything could be invented. Already the seed of a self-created myth was growing in the depths of Adolf's mind.

Needing a safe hideout for times when Munich was too precarious, Adolf selected the Bavarian Alps, with their convenient nearness to the Austrian frontier, across which a skilled mountaineer could guide one in a matter of hours to the nearest haven.

So this mountain house became a retreat for the new political leader and the most trusted of his followers. For more than twenty years, he has nested among the eagles, concocting his monstrous schemes from the height at which the world below seems to be populated only by insensitive insects.

Undoubtedly it was here, incensed by yes-men, impassioned by Putzi Hanfstängl's Bavarian music, that Adolf allowed himself to be persuaded that he was a god among men.

We were approaching Berchtesgaden. At the base of the mountain was a charmingly old-fashioned Bavarian fountain, with wooden figures of Hänsel and Gretel turning round and round. Already the deep pass neighbouring the tiny villages Angela had been describing to me in her prosaic way was broadening into excellent roads. Everywhere buildings were springing from the rocky groves, as though the mountains had burst with some fantastic flower. The coppery sun's lingering rays dazzled against their many windows.

Berchtesgaden was on the way to becoming a modern health resort. A new railroad track was to be laid. Buses would bring hundreds of tourists every day to swell the trade of the no-longer drowsy merchants. But the ubiquitous sightseers would not come to inhale the clear air or enjoy the majestic panorama of the Obersalzberg. The desire would be to drink in the glamour of the greatest myth fabricated outside Hollywood, to bask in the reflected glow of the fabulous entourage, and perhaps to catch a glimpse of the Führer himself.

It was twilight as we began the ascent to Adolf's house along the still none-too-broad winding road, flanked at intervals of about half a mile by houses with signs indicating they catered for transits. At a bend in this road, about two miles from its beginning, the tourist buses halt for their occupants to be shown the narrow drive which winds upwards, for even then Adolf's home was open only to the cars of privileged and invited guests. Townspeople and visitors on foot were still allowed to visit the grounds, but only at certain times, and subject to the discretion of the armed and uniformed men who barred the way and watched like hawks so that no loving subject could approach too near.

After a stop for identification, we began to climb. Later, no such informality was permitted. The same narrow drive became so infested with guards that one seemed to be passing from hand to hand.

This is the only road which leads to the Berghof, as Adolf's villa has been renamed since its new streamlined existence. It would be impossible, or extremely difficult, to scale the precipitous wall of rock, but the defensive system of six miles' radius which encompasses the Führer's residence makes it almost impregnable.

A concrete hut furnished with a guard, a telephone and a machine gun nestles on every tenth rock. Every quarter of an hour the soldier posted there must report – "Nichts neues" (Nothing new) – to the central guard in the Berghof by telephone. At night, further protection is supplied by expertly trained bloodhounds, and even if an adventurous interloper should succeed in eluding the guardsmen and the bloodhounds, he would still have to reckon with the high-tension wires strung from tree to tree like a gigantic and menacing spider's web. Photo-electric cells function like instant antennae to ward off any approach, or registering sound equipment connected with amplifying microphones, so sensitive that one can almost hear the breathing of the night, or the flapping of a raven's wing as it skims this fear-wrought no-man's-land. For Adolf knows only the safety of the transgressor, and his personal enemies are numbered in millions. A special guard is permanently maintained, consisting of 300 hand-picked men under the personal supervision of SA Gruppenführer Brückner, who was responsible for the Führer's safety. Strictest discipline and the fact that his guardians have no way back to lesser eminence other than death, ensure its efficiency, rated even higher than that of the Reichswehr. The slightest carelessness is followed by severe punishment. There can be no errors in this special service: it would take only one wrong visitor allowed to pass the triple defence to kill the Führer.

Since he became Chancellor there must have been numerous attempts on Adolf's life, one of which was made in the Berghof. An SA group leader named Kraus, who was granted permission to present a petition personally to the Führer, was the would-be assassin who came nearest to succeeding. But sitting among the others, waiting to be relieved, he fired at the Führer, as the latter came down the stairs to pass through the hall to the study, and he missed. If he had waited until he was faced with the Führer, the history of the Third Reich might have been quite different. Instead, Kraus's poor timing served to demonstrate the effectiveness of the elaborate defence apparatus. He was killed in less than half a minute. Five guns fired simultaneously.

The motive for his desperate deed can only be surmised. The petition he was bearing was to pardon another SA man, sentenced to three years in prison for homosexuality. It is possible that he wanted revenge for what he may have considered an injustice.

The result of this attack was that additional defensive measures were taken in the presumably invulnerable fortress. Kruas's near-success proved their necessity.

All visitors are required to submit to a search. No revolvers or daggers can be taken into the Berghof. Arms or ammunition of any sort must be deposited at the beginning of the branch leading to the Berghof. Frequently cars were searched again on the way.

Every letter or parcel addressed to the Führer is examined, first in a special room of the Berchtesgaden post house. Only after meticulous scrutiny is it passed on to the mountain top. If anyone managed to mail a bomb (although all post offices inspect suspicious parcels before accepting them), it would explode down in the village.

We halted before a high iron gate, greeted by a chorus of barking Alsatians and shepherd dogs. Angela immediately left the car and motioned us to follow. Brückner's black-uniformed men swept over the Mercedes and poked into every corner. My greatest surprise came when they also went through Angela's luggage and handbag as thoroughly as though she was a stranger. For a moment I thought the head guard was going to search her person as well, but he desisted. When our turn came, however, there wasn't the slightest hesitation. Pat and I were searched as carefully as prisoners.

Once past the barred gate we were soon in front of the house itself. We alighted while the guards drove the car into an adjoining garage, near which was the annexe in which they ate and slept. Adolf's colossal Berghof was still on paper then, not to be projected into steel and glass for some time. The unimposing structure which loomed above us might have been anyone's secluded summer place.

Following Angela, Pat and I entered the brightly lit house. It was quite dark outside by then. Two servant girls, typical Nordic blondes, greeted us with great respect and showed us to our rooms.

The bedroom assigned to me was on the second, or rather top, floor. Not very large, it was comfortably furnished with a modest wooden bed, and furniture of Bavarian design.

As soon as I had settled my things and powdered my nose I returned downstairs, as we had been informed by Angela that supper would be served shortly.

Quick as I thought I had been, Angela was there before me and showed me through the first floor while we waited.

All the rooms were furnished in Bavarian peasant style, comfortably but not lavishly. A room overlooking the garden was panelled with white satinwood. Portraits of the Führer in various poses hung on the wall. There were also a number of enamelled miniatures and assorted paintings, mostly landscapes.

A similar room contained a large radio. Everywhere were National Socialist emblems and tiny flags. Patterned swastikas were on all the cushions, of which there were many, since most of the brightly painted chairs were unupholstered and would have been rather hard without them.

The dining room was the most spacious, with a wide sweep of windows. Around it long wooden seats were built in, with cushions hung on strings from the back and loose ones placed to sit on. In front was the dining table, overhung by a simulated oil lamp, from which a circular wheel without spokes was suspended. This was decorated with marching stormtroopers, cut in wood, some carrying flags, others giving the Nazi salute.

At the end of the room, opposite the window, was a massive stove tiled in green which rose nearly to the ceiling. As a matter of fact all the rooms contained similar stoves, which Angela told me were in frequent use, for even the hottest Alpine days give way to shivering nights. Automatically I put my hand on the smooth glazed surface. It was warm: only then did I realise how chilled I had become during the last hours of our ride. The unexpected heat was welcome.

The table was laid for four. Filling my glass, Angela told me Adolf was expected to join us, even though it was rather late for supper, being nearly ten o'clock. After we had waited for about twenty minutes, a quiet rather sly-looking man came in. He was Schaub, Adolf's adjutant, about whom Pat had told me so much. After a minimum of greeting, he took Angela to one side and began to speak to her in a semi-confidential tone, which was, nevertheless, entirely audible.

"The Führer is asleep," he said as though of a sick person. "And I think it unwise to wake him yet."

"No, no, don't disturb him," Angela hurriedly replied. "Let him sleep."

A few questions and answers completed their

conversation, and Schaub left us. Angela then invited us to sit down and we began to eat. During the first course there was scarcely a word uttered, except when Angela turned to me. "The Führer had a very hard day," she said. "I am very happy that he can sleep."

Without anyone telling me, I had already discovered that you do not comment or ask questions in Germany, it is simply not done. I marvel at how quickly I learned this, for it has always been natural for me to talk with people. Of course, the necessity to communicate in German, particularly the dialect spoken by the Hitlers, contributed somewhat to my becoming an attentive listener rather than a speaker. It was increasingly easy for me to understand, but I found it difficult to reply more than briefly. Perhaps the fact that I came from Dublin, where the most musical English is spoken, had made me particularly sensitive to language. Certainly I did not like to say anything before I knew it was correct. And German is so complicated. While in Germany I became a listener rather than a speaker, and in some obscure way it changed me, for I had never been one to be quiet and listen.

Angela was speaking. "Adolf always had difficulty sleeping. Now more than ever. He is not happy as he used to be.'

After we concluded our somewhat dreary meal, Angela brought out a photo to show us. "Look, Brigette [sic]," she said, handing one of them to me. "This was taken a few months after Geli died. See how sad he looks."

I wondered if showing me the house had brought it all back to her. Geli had been so much on my mind. Maybe she had been on her mother's too. I began to feel sorry for Angela. What bitterness must be locked in her memory.

I looked at the photo. Adolf was dressed in deep

185

mourning, with an expression quite unlike that of any of the portraits I had seen. His eyes were dull and listless. The usually upheld chin was sunk slightly forward. The whole effect was one of cold despair.

Taken all in all it was not a very gay evening. I was glad to retire to my simple Bavarian bed, gladder still that I was there only for a visit.

11

Notwithstanding the fatigue and apprehension I felt when I went to bed in Adolf's house, I woke early, refreshed and, I do not deny it, full of curiosity. As soon as I was dressed I went out on the veranda. This was a wide open porch, which encircled the entire second floor. There was a great deal of curoo-curooing and chirping going on, and I soon discovered the cause of it. A bird-cote was securely fixed to a pole on the side of the house. Several varieties of birds were fluttering around, in the carefree way of birds anywhere in the world.

The view was breathtakingly beautiful. The lonely slopes of living green sank serenely, intersected by the brown ribbon of road we had traversed the night before.

To right and left the majestic Austrian and Bavarian Alps swelled in great undulations, extending into infinity. Behind the house, the mountain, out of which this location had been scooped, towered in rugged grandeur.

A lawn was laid down on the flat surface surrounding the house. In the middle of the garden a telescope mounted on a tripod pointed towards the most remote visible peaks. Across the lawn was a second house for the accommodation of Adolf's special bodyguards.

Sprinkled everywhere were low-growing flowers of a sprightly hue – I learned later that they were cyclamens – which exuded a delicate but insistent fragrance. I drew in deep breaths of the invigorating air. It was a heavenly morning.

I went downstairs, as soon as my watch, as well as my appetite, indicated that it was breakfast time. Pat and Angela were there ahead of me. Angela and I were served boiled eggs, coffee, rolls and marmalade. Pat, however, had bacon and eggs, either because Angela knew his preference, or because of the usual distinction between men and women, which in Germany extends even in such minutiae.

Adolf did not appear.

"It is a lazy day (Faulenzertag)," Angela informed me, and then explained: "Adolf will often remain in bed until noon if he has an interesting book to finish. On such days his breakfast is brought in on a tray and no one is allowed to disturb him."

I asked her if it was true that he never drinks alcohol, and she replied that it was so. For Mittagessen (lunch) Adolf usually has fish or eggs, though guests are frequently served meat. He loves salad. At breakfast he has two eggs in a cup, Schwarzbrot (black bread) and butter with cream cheese and marmalade, and one and a half pints of milk. He particularly likes dessert, which is always served. Fruit pastry with whipped cream or crème caramel and soufflé with whipped cream are frequent dishes.

"And what does he read?" I asked.

Angela smiled indulgently. "Of course he wouldn't like it to be generally known, because everyone thinks he reads only serious work, but he prefers detective or adventure stories. You know, a great man needs distraction, and when he gets started on a good one he can't put it down until he's finished the last page."

I learned from Angela that one of Berlin's well-know publishers of thrillers tactfully stopped the series when the Nazis took over, thinking it unlikely that such books would be welcomed by the Third Reich. It was not long, however, before he was turning out more than before. Far from rejecting them, Adolf had let it be known that this was his wish. Adolf's interest is strictly limited to German books, as he still doesn't read any foreign languages.

"I think he will not be so late today," Angela continued, "because he went to bed early last night. It's only when he's had a trying day that he needs to be alone. Sometimes," she added, "he spends the whole day at the movies. He's changed one of the rooms into a studio. When the new house is built, he will have a special room made that will be marble."

Another interesting detail furnished by Angela is that just as Adolf received a copy of every new book, so every new film is shown to him here. English, Italian and American pictures are presented, as well as German, usually made more understandable by German subtitles. His private cinema is equipped with the most modern sound apparatus. An excellent operator is always available. There is a bell in each of Adolf's hands, so he can see repeats of sequences he specially enjoys.

Adolf is a film fan of long standing, Angela told us. Even when he was still a struggling political agitator, he spent many evenings in the Munich and later Berlin picture houses. If he liked a film especially he saw it about twice or even three times, often on gloomy winter days when time lagged heavily on his hands. He would go from one movie to another. It was not at all unusual for him to witness three full-length programmes before the theatres closed.

"But nowadays," Angela concluded, "my brother is forced to limit his movie orgies somewhat, for his eyes are none too good and he must avoid over-tiring them."

Pat and I decided to walk down to the village. As Angela accompanied us to the door we encountered a man of about 40 who was heading towards the stairs leading to the second floor. When he saw Angela he greeted her with great courtesy, addressing her as Madam Angela. He was Adolf's hairdresser.

Ado was a typical barber, loquacious and amiable. Pat had heard a lot about him and told me Adolf had been shaved by him ever since Ado worked in the Berlin Kurfürstenhof, Adolf's headquarters before he became Chancellor. Later Ado was promoted to the part of 'court barber'. Though Adolf changed, Ado did not. He is the only man who dares joke with Adolf, telling him the same atrocious puns he used to offer his regular customers. He is the most modern equivalent of a court jester. He is allowed to say anything. He collects and tells jokes against his master. He is an amusing fool and a dangerous man.

Ado has his own connections and has gradually wormed his way into an important place in Adolf's entourage, with a single joke that could break careers and ruin men.

As Ado mounted the stairs, Angela looked after him rather angrily. It was not, however, until he was out of sight that she spoke. "Ado has his nose in everything, and repeats all he knows to Adolf. There is no household detail too trivial for him to make something out of. You know how it is, Brigette. When you keep house for any man there are always many little matters you don't mention to him, but Ado does, the swine. He even told Adolf I was helping Herman Göring swindle land from a peasant here. Adolf was furious, thinking he might have Göring for a neighbour – so furious that he made things very difficult for me."

Leaving Angela, we went outside. Crossing the open porch we saw tables and chairs had been set out in front of the big dining-room kitchen window. Probably they had been there before, but I hadn't noticed them in the dark.

After we passed the iron gate with its bars and guards, the road wandered pleasantly down to the village.

It was Sunday, and the melodious ringing church bells invited us to a picturesque Catholic church with a minaret belfry which shared the most important part of the main street with three or four imposing hotels for tourists. Seated on the sidewalk was an artist making sketches.

Inside the church the villagers sat dressed in Sunday garb. The women wore less interesting black dresses and aprons. The men wore short breeches and woollen stockings, which came in two parts, with their bare legs showing between. Many wore flat black hats decorated with gold cord and two tassels. Some had much fancier head-gear trimmed with feathers.

Halfway through the service, as though at a pre-arranged signal, the congregation rose in a body and melted through the doors. Pat and I were nearly the only ones left in the church. When we reached the street it was empty. There were none of the gossiping handshaking groups so familiar on American Sunday mornings.

I looked at Pat questioningly.

"Nazis," he replied simply, as though that explained everything, but went on when he saw I didn't understand. "They don't approve of the people attending Mass, and will do anything to break it up."

We went back up the mountain on a kind of tramway. After a cursory inspection by the guards at the gate, we were astonished to see people clustering in front of the house, from time to time shouting in chorus. "We want to see our Führer, we want to see our Führer." For a moment I wondered how it was possible that they should have so much freedom when we had been so strictly examined.

"Official," Pat said. "Ado told me they're hand-picked by Brückner. Adolf has to be fêted."

"I don't understand."

"It's simple enough, I suppose. Adolf must have applause. Just as someone has to drink, so he has to be worshipped. It's the one thing he had to have."

As we stood there a murmur shimmered through the crowd. "No autographs today." And then a displeased "Ah". But he'd been to the window several times. Would he come again? Apparently not. Finally the group broke up and wandered off, unobtrusively shepherded towards the main gate by the armed guards. We watched them leave. As we were about to go into the house a stumbling young guard came hurriedly towards me bringing a message from the Führer, that he would like to have a talk with me in the garden where he was walking his dogs.

Pat looked at me as though to say, "Be careful, Mother."

I turned to the path which led between the two houses into the garden. I saw my brother-in-law, dressed in the costume of a Bavarian mountain dweller, which consisted of short knickers, which left his knees bare, heavy white stockings, a grey woollen jacket and a green cap. He was greatly changed. When I had last seen him he was poorly dressed and groomed; now he had put on weight and was very well groomed. I thought suddenly of a petit-bourgeois who had won first prize in the sweepstakes and come into possession of everything he'd formerly lacked.

I then walked towards him. He was holding up the heavy whip for three magnificent German Shepherds to jump up. Watching him as intently as I could, without it being too noticeable, I dubiously considered the indisputable fact that my son's and my own life were in the hands of this man, who was so studiously not seeing me. I kept recalling over and over again his last words as the train pulled out with him from Lime Street station in Liverpool: "You'll get everything that's coming to you." Now he had his chance to pay everything back with interest.

It is difficult to deceive a woman; she can always tell when a man is posing. Adolf was a born actor, who played even for a one-person audience. I saw this clearly as he stood there letting me come to him. When I was only a few yards away he ordered the dogs to lie down. One lay at each foot, ears pricked and tails wagging as I approached. Adolf touched them with the whip to make them stop. This made it necessary for him to offer me his left hand, as the right was occupied with holding the whip.

"I hope you are enjoying your visit and are having a good time." He clapped my hand in his and looked at me for a long time. "The years have passed over your head without touching you," he said at last. This was his only allusion to his Liverpool visit. Naturally I didn't comment.

Adolf spoke to the dogs, who eagerly got to their feet, and we began to talk. Adolf presented them to me by

192

name, Blondi, Mack and Wolf (Blondi, his favourite, was later poisoned). He seemed to take great pleasure in their intelligent response to his commands; they understood every inflection of his voice and obeyed like good soldiers. It was interesting to note that he posed for the dogs almost as much for me and equally enjoyed the success with them. They obviously liked him, but dogs, unlike some men, are happy in a state of subservience.

There were innumerable subjects one might have discussed with Adolf, and a thousand questions I might have asked, but I didn't want to sound like a reporter, so I confined myself to uncontroversial subjects. One of the questions I asked, perhaps idiotically, is of wide interest, so I shall include it here.

"Why have you never married?"

For a tense moment I thought I had made a *faux pas*. Perhaps Adolf was touchy on the subject. Perhaps his experience with Geli had given him a complex about women. Perhaps my clumsiness was like salt on a raw wound.

"Do not be embarrassed, Brigette," he said, and his morbid mask assumed a droll but shrewd smile. "You are not the first to ask me that question, and I shall tell you if you are interested. It is a question of statistics. You see, there are approximately 20 million women in Germany, and all of them are more or less attached to me. Then in the Hitler-maid battalions there are approximately 20 million girls being brought up as mine. 20 million women plus 20 million girls equals 40 million Germans. If I were to marry one of these women today, I'd lose the personal interest of 39,999,999 tomorrow. Nine, nine, nine," he repeated boisterously. "I cannot afford to do it." When I laughed he joined in, obviously greatly pleased with himself.

"No woman in Germany must ever be entitled to exclusive possession of me," he went on, as though taking me into his most intimate confidence. "They are charming, the ladies." His tone implied that he and I were worldly friends who could discuss such a matter with safe objectivity. "To love them is a privilege and a pleasure, but to love them too much might prove a pain and a penalty for a man in my position." He smiled at me in as nearly natural way as it is possible for a man who never forgets he must create an impression, even in the relaxation of his own home. "Mein Gott," he exclaimed as though it had just come to him as a great surprise, "I myself cannot explain it, but the women are mad about me. They all love me, and I assure you I do nothing, absolutely nothing, to encourage that sort of thing." He leaned closer. "Can you believe, Brigette, that there are women in Germany who would not wash their hands for a whole week, after shaking hands with me? They say they cannot bear to wash off their Führer's handshake." He grinned engagingly.

"No!" I said. "Not really?"

"Yes," he insisted. "Mein Gott, yes and ..." he paused dramatically. "Göring tells me that when they do wash their hands, these women, they put the water in a bottle and keep it to show their friends."

"That is really amazing," I commented. Adolf let his arms fly in the air as he laughed merrily.

"They are crazy," he said with great satisfaction. "But of course, I am glad to have them feel that way about me."

His enjoyment was jovial but smug. I thought of the matinée idols I had known during my stage career; they too measured their success by the idiocy of their admirers.

"I understand you expressed a desire to settle in our

country." He changed the subject. "I am pleased to hear it. There is no obstacle to that."

As I stood there, a step or two away from him, a thought struck me like a physical blow. Adolf also knew of my conversation with Alois. I had said one word to Alois at his restaurant. A few days later the Chancellor's secretary had a dossier on me, and now the Chancellor was discussing it with me as though it were the most natural thing in the world.

Adolf had begun a discourse on the merits of Germany. Suddenly he interrupted himself, in the middle of a sentence, or word rather, and excusing himself said, in an apologetic tone, "But you will realise all that for yourself, when you become more intimately acquainted with conditions here in Germany."

We started to walk again. Adolf called his dogs, which, tiring of the long pause, had strayed some distance away.

"Angela told me you would like to meet Paula. I would be very grateful to you, Brigette, if you could persuade her to come and visit us." He paused. "She is afraid of me and angry. She doesn't want to understand that she is making herself ridiculous, and me too. Please, Brigette, when you see her, tell her there is room for her here. She could be happy, and if she doesn't want to speak to me she needn't worry that I would force my company on her. Ich habe eine Nebenbeschäftigung auch (I have a second occupation too). I go to Berlin sometimes. Paula could be almost alone here. Or I will build a house for her. I am planning to make changes here. If she once came, I'm sure she'd decide to stay. Do you think you could convince her? I understand she has asked you to meet her at Salzburg tomorrow. I will arrange for you to meet her there."

He stopped walking and looked thoughtful as he said, "Ah, if I could only speak with her and tell her myself, but perhaps you can do it for me." He glanced at the dogs. They were regarding him with great eagerness to be off on what they considered the proper business of the outing. "I must run a little with my dogs. Perhaps it would be better if you returned now." He smiled graciously and accompanied me back to the point from which we started talking of Paula and how absurd she was. He repeated what I had already heard from Angela – that Paula was thinking of writing a book.

I wanted to ask him to let Pat accompany me, but he was already bidding me a courteous farewell. Whistling to the dogs, he turned into a rock-strewn path overgrown with weeds and coarse grass.

12

As I strolled back towards the house, Pat came towards me. I told him Adolf had approved my trip. "But I didn't have a chance to ask him to let you come along."

"You mustn't," Pat began, but broke off quickly. His face indicated nothing of what he was thinking, but instinctively I knew his sudden silence was to avoid giving anything away to the guards in the front of the house. Although they stood as impassive as statues, I realised Pat was right.

Further conversation was prevented by the approach of Angela, who with two maids at her heels had been setting a table out on the open porch. It was nearly lunch time.

We sat down on the porch to wait, having nothing to do – and, truth to tell, I was rather tired, having been on the go all the morning.

After a quarter of an hour we saw Adolf crossing the garden towards the guard's quarters.

Angela told me he always goes out before his own meal to see if the SS guards are satisfactorily provided for. "To create attempts at fellowship," Pat added for my ears.

When we sat down at lunch, we were joined by Schaub and Brückner, who I now saw for the first time. He was a brute of a fellow, as Pat had said, but with handsome features. As Adolf was presenting him to me, another man, about Adolf's age came towards us. He was Amann, a typical German type with a shaved head, whom Adolf addressed as 'Du', the familiar form of 'you', reserved for the family or old friends. He had been Adolf's direct superior in the regiment in which Adolf served during the last war. Adolf was so loyal to him that he even mentioned him in *Mein Kampf*; he also made him director of German publishing.

Scrambled eggs, asparagus swimming in butter, artichokes, Pilze (mushrooms), salad and dessert composed the menu of the meal which was set before us. Angela, like the mother of a great household, served us all without formality. Everything was delicious. We all ate merrily, including Adolf.

I regarded my host. He was bolting his food at what I can only describe as a ravenous rate, as though it were a business operation, to be completed with great efficiency and dispatched as soon as possible. During our earlier encounter I had felt Adolf had become a man of the world, not without a certain manner and air, even though an actor's rather than a gentleman's. Now, however, as he

197

leaned way over his plate to shorten the distance between the food and his mouth, all the time talking loudly and laughing boisterously at the sallies between Amann and Brückner, all poise was dropped and his lack of breeding came through the bluff.

Angela shook her head reproachfully and claimed that he would suffer for eating so fast.

During his earlier years, he told me, he had suffered greatly from indigestion, a condition brought on by gulping his food too quickly, eating at all hours of the day and night, instead of at regular intervals, indulging in fat and greasy sausages, drinking beer and smoking too much, and above all getting over-wrought at his own fiery speeches. When the doctors convinced him that these excesses were making him a wreck, he changed his style.

"Not for himself," Angela commented, "but because he must save his strength for the cause."

The doctors had ordered him to become a vegetarian, teetotaller and non-smoker, and Angela saw to it that he followed their prescription. He has never wavered and he doesn't even drink real coffee, as it is too stimulating, but Hag Kaffee, which contains no caffeine.

On this particular occasion the dessert was Adolf's favourite, consisting of a trifle made with sherry, Austrian-fashion, and smothered with whipped cream. Apropos of the sherry, Angela told me this was the only alcohol he ever indulged in. But this pudding he would not forgo for anything.

Amann had been recounting various anecdotes about Göring, who in Germany, as well as elsewhere, is a favourite target for the whip. One of their stories, new then, goes like this. One day Göring, about to leave home for an official meeting, cannot find his *Pour le Mérite*. The whole house is turned upside down as Göring waits in a fury of impatience in his car. Finally his adjutant comes running, decoration in his hand.

"Where did you find it?" Göring demands.

"It was pinned on your nightshirt, Excellency."

Adolf, laughing loudly, with his mouth open, commented, "No, my friend, I don't think he'll pay ten Marks for that one."

Angela to explain the joke, whispered that Göring always paid ten Marks for a new joke on himself.

It is interesting to note that Göring's self-promoting has been highly successful. In England, and I believe in America too, everyone thinks that among the Nazi gang the most nearly human is Göring. This point of view has been carefully cultivated to make people forget that it was this same fat man who organised and carried out the blood purge in which thousands died. Those who know Germany well rate the smiling Göring as the most dangerous Nazi of them all.

After the meal finally straggled to an end, Adolf suggested that we all go for a stroll. We started out, attended by an athletic young SS guard; he carried blankets and a small hamper of provisions, in case anyone should become hungry on the way.

By this time the sun was shining ferociously. Looking up towards the crest of the mountain which rose loftily over us, I noticed the air was vibrating with haze. We walked so slowly, however, that I didn't tire, and very soon we came to the Königssee, a deep crater-like lake fed by rain water flowing down the sheer cliffs that border it.

We continued through the Malerwinkel (Artists' Corner), which Adolf took pleasure in pointing out to me as the place from which one could get the best view of the lake. He himself had often painted there, he told me, and inquired if I had noticed the paintings he had done of this lake which were hanging in the house. Pausing for a moment, he gazed at the water over which the cliff rim cast its rugged shadow. As he watched broodingly as though lost and oblivious to the others of the party who stood rather awkwardly waiting for him to go on, I felt he was overcome by the romanticism of his own concept of himself. With a quick sigh he turned and walked on for a few yards, and then suggested that we rest. The guards spread several woollen blankets on the ground. Then we all sat down, Adolf asked for Stollen (sandwiches).

Angela, after a careful inspection of the contents of the hamper, prepared several for him and took them to where he sat. Then she also poured out a glass of milk and peeled two apples and an orange for him, before she took any serious interest in the wants of the rest of us.

It was easy to see that Adolf was as dependent on her as is a child on its mother. On this occasion he was completely relaxed and made little jokes, laughed and teased her affectionately. It was difficult seeing this childishly vain man, who so obviously enjoyed being the centre of a small intimate party, to realise that he was the ruthless killer I knew him to be.

I arrived back at the house so tired that I was glad to retire to my room for a nap.

I don't know how long I slept before I woke up. Starting down the corridor towards Pat's room, I met Angela, who suggested that I come into her quarters.

The moment we were inside she began speaking about Paula. It struck me that she was not too pleased that Adolf was expending so much effort to get Paula to come to Germany. I sensed that she and her brother had just been talking about it.

"Paula is the biggest tittle-tattle in creation," Angela said, a little hotly, in the tone of women on women all over the world. "She never seems to know what should be said, and what should be kept quiet. Dear Adolf has struggled so hard to get where he is. You'd think his own sister would realise a man in his position must not be gossiped about. And yet Paula keeps telling silly stories about him. I even heard that she told people he is crazy. Ach, I don't know if it is a good idea for her to come here. She is sure to fight with Adolf if she sees him, but at least she won't be able to talk to outsiders."

Perhaps under ordinary circumstances I might have been amused by Angela's self-revelation, but during my whole visit to Germany there was really only one idea in my mind – how to get myself and Pat out of the country. Angela's intimate tone gave me the kind of confidence I needed to broach the subject of Pat's accompanying me to Salzburg. Even though he had opposed my doing so, I determined to venture it – perhaps by one clever stroke I might succeed in accomplishing the object of his more devious plan.

"I am a little nervous about this trip over the border," I confided to Angela. "In fact, I feel very distressed at the thought of what might happen. I don't like to go alone. What would you think if Pat should go with me?"

Angela's rather petulant expression stiffened into rigidity. "That's entirely out of the question. Willie has been having a few days off, but tomorrow his holiday is over. His name makes it imperative that he be punctual."

"But couldn't you ask?"

"No, Brigette, it's not to be thought of."

Her tone was so definite, I knew it was useless to insist.

Seeking a new topic of conversation, my eyes fell on a copy of *Neues Deutschland* (New Germany), which lay on a small table next to my chair.

"Are you interested in astrology?" I asked, since I knew it was a weekly paper devoted exclusively to that subject.

"Yes," she admitted at once. "I subscribe to four every week.'

"Alois always used to object to my interest," I commented. It was on the tip of my tongue to add that it was I who introduced Adolf to the subject.

"But not Adolf. He never does anything without consulting the astrologers. He has always been interested in the stars and planets. In fact," she added, "he often fetches me out into the garden to look through the telescope, and he has tried to get me to study astrology seriously." She came to an abrupt stop. "Adolf is expecting us in his study. We should go now."

Adolf's study was at the front of the house, next to his bedroom. Angela knocked at the door and we were immediately told to enter. Two men carrying drawings came out as we went in. The room was fairly large and lined with books. Before the window was a large desk, where Adolf was sitting. He was wearing glasses and had changed into a comfortable blue coat with leather buttons, such as the Bavarians wear on weekdays. The material was something like fine satin canvas.

"My plans for enlarging and improving Berchtesgaden," Adolf said, indicating blueprints on his desk.

I glanced at them. Around the original house were added wings and buildings. Adolf pointed to a series of dramatically rendered artist's drawings of the finished project. Rows of pavilions stretched into a town. All the buildings were carved into the rock – underground caves and structures, fully equipped with electric power and sub-surface water systems connected to the super-structure with specially designed elevators.

"Did you design it yourself?" I asked, remembering his 'talent for architecture'.

"Partly," was Adolf's reply, and although he said nothing more, this one word created for me the impression that he had.

When he rolled up the blueprints which had covered his desk and put them away, I noticed that books were neatly piled at both ends. There was a large ornate lamp, and next to it was a photo of Geli when she must have been about twelve years old. A small vase held delicate white flowers. They were Edelweiss (not often available, for it grows only in places hazardous to reach).

The decor was completed by a small statue to 'Germania', holding a torch and a miniature swastika flag.

Angela and I had found places to sit. Pat was ensconced in a cosily cushioned chair when we came in and returned to it. Adolf removed his glasses and turned to me. "Ah, Brigette," he said, "I hear you went to Mass in the village."

I started to comment on the clothes of the parishioners, not wishing to return the ball he'd thrown. But he barely gave me time to finish my sentence, when he was off in his own direction.

"When I was a boy in Austria, when a rich man died they tolled the bells all day, but when a poor man died what did they do?' As Adolf spoke he indulged in the exaggerated mimicry that is second nature to him. First he would be an assiduous bell-pusher. Then he would be pleased to rattle off a few unintelligible phrases, abbreviating the blessing so much that it was scarcely more than a wave of the hand. And then he was serious. "When I have my say, Catholicism's days will be numbered. I will do more good for the German people in a year than all the religious battle has brought in centuries."

I made no reply, but Pat told me later that my expression was such that anyone could have read in it that fireworks would break out in a moment.

Whatever his reason, Adolf jumped off the topic as quickly as he had begun. Pointing to a book at one end of the desk, he asked me if I had noticed what it was. I looked at it and saw that it was a German translation of Carlyle's biography of Cromwell. Taking it in his hand, he handled it almost reverently as he leafed through it.

"What I am today, and what I hope to become," he said after a brief hesitation, "I owe more to these two men than to any other. They were truly great. They placed England two hundred years ahead of any other European power." He paused briefly. "My own life is an exact parallel of Oliver Cromwell's. He too recruited his army from among the people and after the overthrow of the aristocracy gave the reins of government back to the people."

Adolf went on enthusiastically about the glories of England. "I would have to admire her, if for no other reason, because she produced Carlyle – one of the greatest philosophers of all time. Unfortunately," he added, "she is being poisoned from within by opportunists. She will never be able to attain her old position in the world, if this is not quickly stopped."

I asked Adolf whether he thought Cromwell's messages were better than those of Napoleon.

"Both men handled the situations which arose as seemed best at the time. In many ways I believe Cromwell's solutions were better. Of course, Cromwell was completely forgotten after his death, because he was unable to keep or consolidate his power."

"As Napoleon did by having himself crowned Emperor?"

Pat asked.

"That was one way, of course."

For the first time Angela entered the conversation, turning to me with a rather condescending smile.

"Did you know, Brigette, that Adolf was offered the crown of Bavaria? They even took the crown jewels from Nuremberg."

"That is not to be discussed, Angela," Adolf reproved, giving her a stern look; but he was not loath to explain that as he was head of the German Workers Party such a step was entirely out of the question. "And, in any case, I will consolidate my strength without resort to such old-fashioned methods."

On this note Adolf stood up, letting us know that the visit was over. As Angela started to come with us, Adolf asked her to remain. Her "Yes, Adolf" was exactly like the acquiescence of a child about to be scolded.

Pat and I decided to walk in the garden, so we could talk. When I told him of my conversation with Angela he was very disturbed, though he tried not to let me see how much.

"What a pity you said that. Now you will be suspected and I shall be worse off."

Further discussion was prevented by Angela, who was coming towards us swiftly.

"Brigette," she began at once, "I told Adolf you were

worried to go alone. He will send someone in whom you can have perfect confidence to help you cross the border."

"Thank you, Angela," was all that I could say.

When we were alone, Pat said: "You see, now you'll have someone to go with you, and you know who that someone will be – one of the guards. That's bad. They are all chosen and sworn in by Adolf himself. There will be only the ghost of a chance that you can do anything."

"But how can Adolf send guards into Austria? It's a foreign country."

Pat looked at me as a sophisticated man of the world at an innocent girl. "You believe that?" he said. "You have no idea how well he has organised everything." His tone was discouraging as he went on. "If only you didn't have to be involved in this affair. I'm helpless to get you out of it. Any action I might take would only make it more dangerous for you. So long as they don't know our plan, you'll be all right – I think, but I don't know for sure. That's why I wished you hadn't said anything to Angela about me, if they're suspicious."

"Well, Pat, I'll just have to do the best I can and put my trust in God."

"And Paula," added Pat. "The only thing to do is to place yourself under her protection, if she dares go as close to the German border as Salzburg she must have taken every precaution. But promise me, whatever happens, that you will try to get away from Adolf's men. They are not the type to hesitate at anything, even to shoot you. But I still think we'd better risk it. And don't think that because everyone has been so polite to you the danger is only in my mind."

It was time for Pat to take the night train back to Berlin. When we said goodbye and I watched him go, a feeling of great depression came over me. That night, alone in the enemy's house, I scarcely slept at all. The balsam air no longer invigorated me, and the dark mountain that towered behind the house seemed sinister rather than majestic.

As I lay in bed staring out into the mysterious night, a chill crept around me. It had all sounded quite simple when Pat and I had discussed my chances of escape. And the Hitlers had seemed so gemütlich at this afternoon's picnic. Yet the horrors taking place in Germany were no longer remote: every minute I had been there, they came closer. I thought of Geli, the only human being my brother-in-law had loved: she was dead, and the Germany he claimed so fervently to adore was dying. The silence of the mountain which had seemed so tranquil and beautiful was now like the silence of death. Uneasily I wondered what the future would hold for Pat, for me, for my strange family by marriage.

13

The next afternoon, when I left Berchtesgaden to drive to Salzburg, it was in the company of two young men dressed in civilian clothes.

Far from being sinister in aspect, my two escorts were young, blond and insistently charming. They even tried to speak English with me, evidently finding this a good occasion to improve their vocabulary. The one who sat in the rear with me had a small dictionary and kept referring to it for phrases to try out; it was awful. After only a little of this I begged them not to be so polite, but it was only with great difficulty that I got him to leave me alone.

We arrived at the border at about three o'clock and passed without difficulty.

A short time later our car arrived in Salzburg, in front of the Hotel Goldner Hirsch in the Getreidegasse near the River Salzach, where I was to meet Paula. The youth who sat in the back helped me out; the other who had driven the car joined us. Thus I entered the hotel lobby flanked on both sides by Hitler's bodyguards.

When we inquired about Paula at the desk, the clerk called her room and informed us that she wished us to sit down in the lobby, where she would soon join us. We must have been waiting for about ten minutes when four civilians entered the lobby from the street door. After a brief exchange of words at the inquiry desk, they turned and came directly to us. Announcing that they were Austrian state police, they politely asked to see our passports. When I showed the chief my Austrian one he merely said "Thank you" and turned to examine the others. I don't know what irregularities he found, but it was enough to require further investigation.

My escorts protested vigorously, but the police insisted the Germans accompany them. They left, and nearly at the same moment I saw a woman who distinctly resembled Adolf come out of the elevator.

Paula's resemblance to her brother is startling. She has the same round-cheeked face and protruding nose. Only about the mouth is there a discernible difference. It is easy to see she never laughs. The mouth was not designed for laughing; her lips are always tightly compressed. Hers was the face of a woman who had been frustrated all her life. Her expression showed solemn dissatisfaction with the world in general and herself in particular.

I tried to thank her for disengaging me from my unwanted escorts, but she brashly interrupted me.

"It means nothing. You were unimportant to them. They were after me. During the last few years scarcely a month has passed without at least one attempt on Adolf's part to drag me off to his beautiful house in the mountains. But I refuse to go. It is only a token payment for everything Adolf has done to me."

Paula had already checked out of the hotel, but she asked me to wait for a few moments while the porter arranged for her luggage. He came a few moments later, and Paula drew him aside and questioned him sharply. As the conversation lasted several minutes I had the distinct impression that there was more to it than appeared. In fact, I was sure he had been her accomplice in this exposing of the guards, though how that little affair was engineered I had no idea.

We took a cab and half an hour later I was seated opposite Paula in a second-class compartment of the Vienna train.

Almost before we were comfortably seated Paula began complaining about Adolf and his neglect of her. She had never forgiven him for the twenty years during which he didn't bother to find out whether she had a roof over her head or anything to eat. The corners of her mouth sagged, and her thin upper lip crinkled as she spoke of Adolf. For a moment I thought of Alois, curious how much affected these Hitlers were by each other's selfishness and how thoughtless one was of the other.

Throughout the journey Paula kept on talking. She gave me the impression of being a lonely and bitter woman, who seldom had the chance to confide in anyone. She was not the type to talk to strangers, so I suppose I must have come as a needed audience. She talked and talked, the words pouring from her lips as a river overflows its banks and floods the countryside. And her words seethed with hatred.

"And if I could forget all the harm Adolf has done me in the past," Paula said implacably, "how could I forgive what he has done and is doing against Christ and the Church?"

It was not by accident, Paula continued, that priests everywhere were being thrown in prison on the slightest pretext, or merely because they mentioned such cardinal points as the Immaculate Conception in their sermons. In Oldenburg, she told me, Adolf ordered that all the crucifixes be removed from the churches and that religious teaching be stopped. On the day the order was carried out thousands of outraged citizens took part in a demonstration at the town hall. The protest was on such a grand scale that the governor of the province, who had initiated the order, promised that the crucifixes would be restored, and they were. In the meantime, however, the authorities had found out the names of the ringleaders. All were arrested within a week; the next of kin received postcards informing them that if they would meet such-and-such a train they would receive the ashes of the arrested men.

"It is Adolf's insatiable vanity that has led him into this madness," Paula insisted. "What man in his right senses can believe himself the reincarnation of our Saviour, as Adolf does? That's why he hates the Church, because it will not tolerate his sacrilegious attempt to beatify himself. He would have had himself declared God by now, if it were not for the strength of the Catholic Church. Already he has established Hitler churches."

Paula's voice was that of a denunciating fury as she spoke. "A painting of my brother, the Anti-Christ, hangs before their altars. On each side burn unholy candles. *Mein Kampf* is their bible. Couples are married and children baptised with ritual fire. When they leave the church they are handed a copy of his blasphemous book. Like wildfire his evil has spread through the land. They mean to discredit Christianity and bring back to Germany the pagan beliefs of two thousand years ago. This year they made the Sonnenwendfeuer (at midsummer) at the beginning of summer, and in a few days there will be another heathen holiday when it ends. All through the length and breadth of Germany they hold meetings. You can see the flames of their log fires for miles. I know what they are doing, these devil worshippers. May they all die by fire and sword."

I needed very little of this to realise that Paula was just as violent in her personality as her brother. It just happened that they were on opposite sides.

Her devotion to my son, who had been the only one in the family to take a kindly interest in her, promoted me to a place of trust. At least, I suppose that's why I became the recipient of her intimate confidences.

The history of that amazing family, as if projected on a screen, passed before my eyes during our trip. There appeared the founder of the dynasty, Alois Schicklgruber; he bore his mother's old name because he was the illegitimate child, adopting the name of Hitler only in middle age. When he was an old man he always carried a whip in his hand, terrifying his family every time he entered a room in which they were gathered. I thought of Adolf and his whip.

The most serious crime in the eyes of Adolf's father was

laziness. He could not bear to see one of his children sitting quietly without some occupation. The daughters, Angela and the youngest child Paula, had to take up sewing and knitting immediately after the housework was done. Paula told me she was never allowed to go out at night, even after Angela was married. "I know that sort of thing," her father would say. "One goes out and two come back."

"Once," Paula told me, "Adolf, who so often played hookey from school, had built a little boat of odds-and-ends and took it down to the river. When our father heard of it he followed Adolf, snatched up the boat and smashed it to pieces. Then he grabbed Adolf by the throat and held him against a tree, until he half-choked. Adolf dropped in a faint. Only then did the old man wake up to what he was doing; he picked Adolf up and carried him home. For a week Adolf was more dead than alive."

Their father had one absorbing interest, politics. When he came home from his office, his wife would take off his shoes and put on his house slippers. Then he would reach for the newspaper and immerse himself in it until dinner time. Sometimes, too, he would go to the inn where, at the traditionally reserved table, he discussed politics with other tavern politicians. He liked to tell stories of the war of 1866, which he'd helped fight and lose for the Austrians. He was an impassioned Austrian, hated the Prussians and despised Bismarck. Sometimes he spoke of the Emperor Francis Joseph, whose hand he had been permitted to shake at some public function. He hoped that eventually Austria would again go to war with Germany. Then we'd show Prussia who was the stronger.

"Adolf was never a healthy child." Paula continued. "His lungs were weak. Twice he was stricken with pneumonia and recovered only through some miracle."

All the more important, therefore, it seemed to his mother to select for him a career with which he could cope physically. She decided he should become a civil engineer and succeeded in persuading her husband to use all his money for Adolf's training and education. Alois, my husband, was to learn the restaurant business. That required no fee.

His mother spoiled Adolf. If other boys gave him a licking he'd run home crying and Alois would have his ears boxed, because he hadn't come to Adolf's rescue and taken a beating for him.

Adolf was the weakling, and behind in school. He was a difficult child, indifferent to everything around him. Towards Angela and Paula he behaved abominably, always threatening them with blows and pulling their hair.

One thing which he inherited from his father was his love of uniform. If his father was out, Adolf would sneak into his room, put on his uniform jacket and with a wooden sword march through the garden. In a loud voice he'd shout military commands, salute and demand a salute from an imaginary passing subordinate. His favourite games were court-martial and execution afterwards.

After his father's death Adolf became altogether apathetic. Mostly he stayed in bed until late in the afternoon, and then only got up to wander down the river. There he would sit for hours motionless, chewing a straw. Occasionally he drew a little, or painted pictures in watercolours. His mother did not like that. She was convinced that one could not earn one's living painting. Another source of worry to her was the fact that Adolf ate irregularly and preferred a piece of cake or a tart to substantial food. In the evening he locked himself in his room as a rule, and read late into the night. His reading consisted exclusively of adventure stories, set in America or Asia. Thrillers written for children of ten or twelve he read over and over again until he literally knew them by heart.

When his father died, Adolf and Paula were the only ones to remain with their mother. She lived until Adolf was nearly twenty. Then everything was sold and they both went to Vienna to stay with Angela. After Adolf left there, Paula heard nothing from him. He didn't even bother to write. For a long time she thought he was dead. When years later he invited Angela to come live with him, she was glad enough to go – but not Paula.

"Perhaps," Paula said grimly, "one day I might have changed my mind, but when he killed Geli there was no question. The only thing that keeps me from publicly accusing him is the memory of our mother. I would accuse him of the deliberate murder of Geli. And don't misunderstand me. I'm not saying that he drove her to death, caused her to commit suicide, or anything like that. I mean to accuse him of shooting and killing her."

"But have you any proof?" I asked her.

"Have I any proof?" She looked at me almost reproachfully for not accepting her words at their face value. "I have enough proof to convince a fair jury that Adolf should be convicted of murder." She made the sign of the cross.

"He was in love with her, his own niece. When I heard about it I begged Angela to send Geli to me in Vienna. According to Angela the gun went off by accident while the two of them were struggling. It was in Adolf's hand."

"But that's not the story Angela told me in Munich," I interrupted.

"Naturally not. She was obliged to tell everyone it was suicide. Göring arranged all that, even tried to make it appear Adolf wasn't there when it happened."

"And what about the story that Geli was pregnant. Was that true?"

"Not a word of truth in it. That fiction was circulated by Göring to establish a possible motive for suicide. Angela had always protected Adolf and found excuses for him. And it's difficult to find an excuse for a man who brandishes a revolver during a discussion with a member of his own family, in his own home. Ach! What a fool she is, Angela. Adolf twists her right round his little finger, the way he did my mother. No matter what he does, she stands up for him and turns everything to make him look right. It was a scandal that he should be running around with Geli, but Angela let it go on. Then when he killed her, she passed it off as suicide. And now she gets sentimental about how attached she was to the child. If she had let Geli come here, she could have married and settled down, but now she's dead and Adolf has bad dreams."

I was amazed. This woman who had no communication with the family knew all the details of what happened in Munich. I asked her how she knew.

She replied without any effort at concealment that she had learned about it from the Austrian government's file. The evidence collected by Gerlich was well known to them.

"What do you think will happen to my son?" I had tried again and again to put the question to her during our long conversation. Now at last she replied.

"You needn't worry," she said in deliberate tones. "I'm going to get him out of there."

"But suppose it takes too long. At any moment he may be in danger," I insisted.

"Don't worry. I'll make Adolf understand that your son is under my protection. If any harm comes to him, I have enough proof of the things I say, that if I wanted to make them public it would ruin Adolf. You may rest assured that whatever I promise, I do."

"Thank you, Paula, and you must excuse a mother for being anxious about her son, but what would happen if …" Again she didn't allow me to finish my sentence.

"What would happen if Adolf should get me into his power? You don't have to think about it. I'm taking care of myself, and so are the Vienna police. Still it is better to be prepared for anything when you are fighting a madman." Paula's voice came to an abrupt stop. She began to speak again – her tone was entirely changed. "In his way, I suppose Adolf loves me. I am his real sister. But he has this insane obsession."

"Tell me, Paula," I asked her, "are you going to write a book on Adolf?"

Paula stared at me surprised. "How do you know that? It's supposed to be a secret."

"Well," I replied, "if it's a secret, it's a badly kept one. Both Angela and Adolf know about it, and spoke of it to me."

"How he found out I don't know," Paula said. "I had scarcely made up my mind, and he's heard of it already." She paused for a moment before continuing in her earlier tone. "Adolf is afraid of me because I am in possession of all the facts, including the origin of our family, which he would like to suppress. You see, Brigette, in the book that Adolf wrote, *Mein Kampf*, he gave an absolutely misleading picture of his family. According to him, our parents didn't come from Austria, but from a Bavarian family. This was absolutely false, and he never mentioned that Father married three times, or that he had brothers and sisters. According to *Mein Kampf*, Father and Mother lived happily together and he was their only child. Of course the members of the family are living refutations of a statement he made in his book. Since it has now become practically the Bible of the German people, our existence is a serious handicap. Ten years ago Adolf said we didn't exist. Now he can't well deny what he wrote in *Mein Kampf*. Of course he is the dictator now, but that doesn't make it any less annoying. Particularly since he started the race laws, we have no grandfather, Adolf and I. Certainly anyone who wished could make a good deal out of that."

While Paula was speaking I was thinking, perhaps egotistically, of my son. I said to her: "Please, promise me you won't publish this book until after my son leaves Germany."

"Very well, Brigette," she agreed after a moment. "And thank you for telling me Adolf knows about it. It was simple enough for him to find out, I suppose. Austria is full of his agents. He has sent I don't know how many here. One time or another they have searched every registrar's office, every parochial office, every archive that might contain documents relating to our family, and everything they found they destroyed. Some papers were burned. Others were taken away. They haven't succeeded in obliterating Adolf's tracks entirely, because Dollfuss also kept a dossier. It's my opinion that that's why he was killed. You know, many people who have been too curious or too well informed about Adolf died in the 1934 Berlin purge."

I stayed two days in Vienna, as Paula's guest. Shortly after our arrival we wrote to Pat. Knowing that Adolf would read the letter, it was designed more for him than my boy.

First of all I related the deplorable incident at Salzburg, describing it in such a way as to divert suspicion from Paula. I said that Paula was ill and that I couldn't permit her to travel back to Vienna alone, so I accompanied her there, and in order to erase any possible mistrust from Adolf's mind I added that it was my intention to stay with Paula a few days, and then 'return to London to liquidate my affairs, for it was my intention to settle down on the Continent for good'.

I handed the letter to Paula for her approval, excusing myself for the many lies I had told on paper.

"It's Adolf," she commented bitterly. "When we were children my mother often scolded me for lying, and many time I heard her say, 'This child is so adept at lying, she can twist herself out of any scrape.' She blamed my father's unreasonable severity for it. Now it's the same in all Germany. Everyone has to lie to escape Adolf."

During the few days I stayed with Paula in Vienna, I really came to like this strait-laced old maid who had lived all those years in puritanical poverty in the same tiny third-floor flat on the Schönburgstrasse, in which she had lived with Angela when she first came to Vienna after her mother's death. I slept in the alcove on a folding bed she told me Adolf used to occupy when he stayed with the Raubals – a folding metal bed, a shabby relic of the Führer's past.

14

After my adventure in Germany and Austria I kept up a regular correspondence with Paula, who was my only source of information about Pat. And her letters to me – unlike his – were not subject to Adolf's censorship. It was through her I learned what was happening to Pat, and how he managed to carry on. She had her own sources of information – I don't know what they were, but through them she always managed to get news.

Paula's letters were, without exception, reassuring. In every one of them she told me that Pat was all right and that I need not worry. As opposed to these reassurances, however, the letters I received from my son instilled in me an ever-growing fear. The last line in each was the same: 'When are you coming back? Don't forget you promised me you would come here to live.' This message affected me so powerfully that I felt like packing and starting off on the forbidden journey, although I knew these words were for the censor and Adolf, not for me. Each time I read them it was all I could do to restrain myself from doing what I knew I must not.

Thinking of those days, I recall the many strangers with vague errands who rang my bell and sought by devious means to gain my confidence. Now I am sure of what at that time I didn't even suspect, that they were sent by Berlin to keep track of me. I would have pooh-poohed the idea that a great state like Germany would bother to send agents to London, simply to check up on an ordinary woman like me, but now it is common knowledge that a well-organised Gestapo agency found no detail of British life too minute to be interesting. It is to Mr Rudolf Olden, the brilliant biographer, that I owe thanks for warning me of this danger.

Like thousands and thousands of others, Rudolf Olden was a martyr to Hitlerism. At the beginning of the war when he was on the way to America to publish his new book about Hitler, the ship sank.

At the time of which I am now speaking – 1937 – Olden

was working on this book. He came down from Oxford to see me when he learned that I had returned from my trip to Berchtesgaden. And we had a number of long visits, in which I recounted my personal experiences.

One of the subjects in which he expressed particular interest was the death of Geli. When I told him all I had heard, Olden looked at me oddly. Then he said: "In Adolf Hitler's case, the truth of Oscar Wilde's saying that 'they kill the thing they love' is once more demonstrated. And his niece is not the only one. No doubt you must have heard of Renate Müller."

"The film actress?"

"Yes. Well, she's dead too."

Renate Müller, Olden told me, was a lovely blond, not unlike Geli in appearance, but more polished. Adolf first saw her in a screen version of Faust. She played the part of Marguerite, which was the perfect vehicle to convey her peculiar quality of charm to the Führer.

Brückner, Hitler's adjutant, was dispatched to invite her to tea at the Chancellery in Berlin. And later she became a frequent visitor to Berchtesgaden. For a time they saw a great deal of each other, it even began to look as if Adolf might marry her. But after a while Adolf became moody and suspicious. Renate tried to pacify and reassure him. He was foolish to be jealous of her work, she said. An actress, she would repeatedly tell him, must meet men, must spend hours rehearsing, making up, working.

But Hitler's suspicions increased. His insults grew more savage, his accusations more direct. It was impossible for her to please him.

A trip to France in the spring included the Riviera. There she met an actor, not very young, not very talented, not even well-known. She fell in love with him; she was indiscreet enough to kiss him in the walled garden of a pension, near Cannes where they both were guests.

The weekend after Renate Müller returned she was invited to Berchtesgaden. The other guests scarcely saw her. She was closeted with the Führer in his study. The man who had been so kind and so interested in her career questioned her on her trip. Had it been a success? Had she arranged all the business satisfactorily?

"Yes, my Führer," she must have said. "Yes."

It must have been then that Adolf showed her the photograph of herself and her lover kissing in the garden which Nazi agents had managed to snap. At the end of the session he sent her away, telling her he never wanted to see her again.

Later she received a letter. She might know what the letter said: she would never play in German leading pictures again.

Olden added: "She was forbidden to earn a living in Germany in the only way she knew how, and she was forbidden to go elsewhere. There were, I heard, two hours between the arrival of the letter and the finding of her crumpled body in a courtyard. She had fallen out of a window. No one knows how it happened."

"Poor girl," I said. "It's another Geli story."

Another topic we discussed at some length was the subject of Adolf's responsibilities. I should like to say here unequivocally that I do not hold with the theory that Adolf was a poor deluded neurotic who has been propped up by the gangsters behind him and led unwittingly into committing the crimes he has against individuals and mankind.

In my opinion Adolf is an arch-hypocrite, perhaps the greatest of them all. He has always carefully arranged it so that he is not personally to blame for the deeds committed in his name. He was undoubtedly preparing right now the excuses for every crime he has perpetrated in the name of Germany.

"It is not I," he will say, "but the German state which did this and that. I ask it in the name of the German people. I was easily elected by the vote of the German people. For myself I have done nothing."

He is the master of the art of the double-cross and is just as ruthless with his family and friends as he has been with the Poles, for example. He is as much of a mystery man to his followers as to the Americans, except in cases where they 'have something on him'. Schaub, Streicher and Göring are understood to be in the enviable position Röhm probably was, but Röhm is dead.

Although I think it is a great mistake to overrate Adolf, I think it is an even greater one to underestimate him. Above all he is a confident actor with method in his greatest madness.

One day Mr Olden was with me when a visitor arrived, a man whom I didn't know. He presented an excellent letter of recommendation from an acquaintance of mine and said that he was sent by Pat. Naturally I received him gladly and listened eagerly to what he told me. He was a member of the Black Front, he confided, an anti-Nazi organisation which still operates in Germany. He had come to discuss with me a plan of Pat's for breaking off his connections in Germany and returning to England.

I was delighted and hurried into the next room in which Olden was waiting to tell him the good news.

The moment I was through the door, he took me by the arm. He was a very tall man and had to lean down to reach my ear.

"My God," he whispered, "do you know who your visitor is? He's a Gestapo agent. He is the same man who kidnapped Streicher, the famous Berlin journalist."

Stunned by this warning, I returned to my visitor to play the role of sister-in-law of the Führer. I was astonished, I told him, that he should think my son would want to leave Germany, where his future was assured. As soon as I could, I ushered my guest out, thanking the good fortune that brought Rudolf Olden to my house that day. I never saw the Nazi again.

After this adventure I knew what to say to anyone who might come, and really I had no fears for my own purposes. Surely they would not venture to do me any harm, but at night when I lay awake a thousand fears about Pat swarmed in my mind. I could not overcome the bothering thought that things were going badly with him.

And then came a day which I shall never forget. It was a grey English day, the fog sat solidly on the street, and seemed almost to creep under the doors and around the window frames.

My friend Mr Olden had been there, but had left, and a bitter depression had settled over me. Painful as the fog, I had no strength left to pretend to myself I was not in despair. Everything seemed hopeless and worthless.

Suddenly the bell pealed, again and again with an impatient vigour. Only Pat rang the bell like that; it was his signal. When I opened the door I was gripped in an embrace of steel. Only a young and happy man could have spoken the carefree gay words which pierced my ear.

"How on earth did you get here?" I asked.

"As a matter of fact I'm not here," he began jokingly. "I'm really on a boat touring Norway."

"Be serious," I urged him.

"I am. All German employees are listed to take part in trips organised by the Kraft Durch Freude. My name was down for Norway, and I embarked with a few hundred others. When we docked, everyone went ashore to take photographs. I just didn't get back to the boat on time." He laughed exuberantly, and added, "I wasn't the only one either, but the others were pretty annoyed to have to wait two weeks for the boat to come back, that's all. So here I am."

"Won't they do anything to you?"

"What can they do? I am a British citizen."

"But how did you get money to come home?" I asked him.

"I sold my family. Now give me something to eat. You can't imagine how much I thought of our good meals at home."

I watched Pat as he devoured the food I hurriedly set out. There was something that had puzzled me about the way he looked. Now for the first time it came to me what it was. He had completely lost the harassed expression his face had worn in Berlin. He was sure and confident. It was almost too good to be true. All our problems were solved. We could begin a new life.

It was wonderful to have Pat home. That first day we talked for hours, talking over our adventures and comparing notes. Pat questioned me at length as to how I was getting on. He couldn't believe that I had a good situation and was comfortably established. Naturally I wanted to know all about what had happened in Germany since I had left. But Pat was curiously reticent. He told me innumerable anecdotes with avid candour, but when I thought about them later they didn't add up to a complete picture.

He had left the Reichskreditbank and worked in the Opel automobile factory. Later, he had been an automobile salesman. He led a very gay social life. He met many theatrical people.

I turned all these facts over in my mind and came to the conclusion that I knew little or nothing of the worldly young man who was staying with me.

During the week that followed I scarcely saw Pat at all. He was very busy. I assumed he was arranging his affairs with the authorities, or looking for work.

One afternoon, when he was out, I took a telephone message that a Mr Fenton wished to speak to him. When Pat came home hours later, I relayed the message to him, wondering what he would say.

He was a bit embarrassed. "Yes, I know," he commented hesitantly. "I saw him this afternoon, about a book I was planning to write."

Something in his tone made me uneasy, and I questioned him more persistently than I would ordinarily have done. "A book? I didn't know you were writing a book."

"You see, Mother," he began, and then took a deep breath as if before a dive. I knew something important was about to be divulged, it was his 'explaining voice.' "I haven't been quite frank with you. In four days the Kraft Durch Freude boat will stop at the port where I got off, on its way to Germany. I have to rejoin the group and go back."

For a moment I was so surprised the breath seemed to be knocked out of me. "But are you mad? You can't be serious. After all the trouble you had, you want to return – why?"

Pat's reply was so vague and roundabout that I quickly brushed it aside. "Only the truth," I demanded.

"It doesn't make sense." And then a new idea struck me. "Or did you leave someone there – is it a girl?"

"That's it, Mother." He pounced on my words. "Don't you remember? The girl I pointed out to you in the Winter Gardens. She's ..."

But I knew already he was fabricating the whole thing. The eagerness with which he grabbed at the explanation I offered, the relief on his face when he thought he'd found an argument, were too transparent ...

"Tell me the truth," I responded. "What you are trying to make me believe is nonsense, and you know it. And anyway, who is this Fenton who was so serious with me over the telephone?"

"Listen to me, Mother. There is a girl," he began, not answering my question about Fenton. "She couldn't come with me, and even though I love her I couldn't do anything about it at the time, but now I've thought of a way I might be able to get her out." He paused, obviously at a loss as to how to continue, but before I could say anything, he was stumbling on. "You know, Mother, it was my idea to write a book. I went to discuss it with some people I thought ought to know about it and help me in case of any difficulty."

I stared at Pat. Book? Fenton? It was such a jumble I was completely confused. Why should Pat go back to Germany? What was he going to do there? And then an astonishing, though inevitable, speculation insinuated itself into my mind. Perhaps he had been engaged in some activities I knew nothing about. Perhaps he could have come home at any time, but chose to remain.

"Some people," I found myself saying thoughtfully. "What people?"

Pat hesitated again before he answered. Then he

spoke very quietly. "I wish I could tell you all about it, but that's out of the question. Anyway, it's better for you not to know."

We both fell silent. When one can't ask questions and the other won't answer, there's not much to talk about. I began mentally turning over the details and examining them.

"Isn't it dangerous for you to go back?" I hazarded finally. "You ran away from the boat. Won't that arouse suspicion?"

"On the contrary," Pat laughed, not without relief at my apparent acceptance of the situation. "If I was under the slightest suspicion before and now I return, after having been a free man for a week, what could anyone say? I arrive back in Germany on the same boat. All suspicion will be averted."

"You are just crazy," I told him. "You are forgetting you're already a condemned man. You told me yourself."

"Oh, you know," Pat interrupted smiling, "that was when you were there. Everything was different then."

For everything I said Pat had an answer. I saw he really meant to go, and though I didn't for one moment believe it was as simple as he claimed, I was beginning to run out of arguments.

And then a strange thing happened. Ever since we had been mixed up with this hateful German affair I had felt as though we'd been pushed into it and were being tossed hither and thither in a vast chaotic sea of activity. But Pat's attitude was changed. All I needed was one glance at him to realise that he was as full of purpose as a dog after a bone. No one had been pushing him around now for a long time, I was sure of it; and with that certainty came the impression that he had been remaining in Germany of his own free will, and that now he was deliberately returning to carry out business of a very definite nature. It was almost as though a powerful lens was focusing before my eyes.

"Look here, Pat," I told him, "I don't know what you've been up to, and I see you won't tell me, but if you're going back into that poisonous country after all that's happened in it to you, I hope you have a good reason."

When Pat saw I was not to be put off, he took me in his arms and spoke to me with great seriousness. "Brigette, Mother, please trust me. I have to go. No matter what you say, I would still have to go. But please don't ask me any more than that. But don't worry, nothing will happen to me."

There was no more to be said. The remaining days telescoped into the moment for Pat's departure.

As he was packed and ready to go he pressed a small key into my hand. It was his key for our safe-deposit box at the bank, in which we locked all our documents, letters and information we had gleaned on the Hitler family and their activities. Pat made me promise to see that no harm came to these records. "They may be of vital importance one day," he said, emphasising each word. But he needn't have, for I could see from his manner that he was serious.

"All right, Pat," I sighed, "and don't worry about my end of things. Only before you go I wish you would tell me if you're going there to be a … I mean, how should I say it – are you going there to get information for the government? I can keep a secret."

"Oh no, Mother, don't say that. Whatever you may think, never say one word to anyone, unless you wish to do me an injury. It is much better for both of us that you know nothing."

An irresistible impulse collapsed, momentarily. "I don't know," I said to him, "but it seems to me that you're always managing to get us into the most complicated situations."

Pat hugged me, once again his old beaming self. "You have only yourself to blame," he said. "After all, it was you who got me into this. If it hadn't been for your romancing, I might have been an Irish farmer." We both laughed.

He picked up his bags and was gone, stopping once to wave from the corner. He had forbidden me to go to the station with him.

15

A month passed. There was no word from Pat. The assurance I had felt the day of his departure was wearing thin, and then I began to hear from him. He was well, work was the same as always, nothing was happening. They were the same old letters all over again, written more for the censor than for me.

I tried to convince myself that all was going well. The fact that I'd heard from him must prove that he hadn't been suspected. But what new dangers might be threatening him? Into what traps might his new work lead him? And then began the period I shall never forget, the Austrian papers began to print frenzied articles on the 'German Question'. Europe was in an uproar.

On 8 February 1938, there was a great shifting of heads of departments in Berlin. The Foreign Office acquired a new chief, Ribbentrop. War Minister and Minister of Reichswehr were changed. In the English papers these events were described as the 'bloodless purge'.

On 12 February, Austria moved into the foreground. Schuschnigg, the Austrian Chancellor, went to Berchtesgaden, to confer with Adolf. The press candidly declared that the independence of Austria could not last more than a day.

On 11 March, Schuschnigg announced that the Führer had sent him an ultimatum, to which he had no other choice but to bow, permitting German troops to occupy Austria.

The next day we were obliged to learn a new German word, Anschluss. Like all the new words that were coming from Nazi Germany, it was a lie. The dictionary gives it meaning as 'a coming-together, or joining'. The Nazi meaning of the word, however, is the occupation of a peaceful neighbouring state, without a declaration of war, but with planes, tanks and I don't know how many divisions of men.

London was in a fine state of excitement. I remember discussing the latest developments with a friend, who said he couldn't make up his mind on whom to place the blame, Hitler or Schuschnigg, although he felt inclined to choose the latter. After I'd thought a little, I realised he was right. Schuschnigg, whom we sadly remember as the last Austrian Chancellor, was entirely undeserving of sympathy. When he saw that Austria was menaced by Nazism, instead of making his country an advanced post of democracy he installed a semi-Fascist regime and entered into competition with Hitler. This competition, or perhaps I should say imitation, extended into the most amazing detail. He adapted an Austrian swastika; 'Heil Hitler' became 'Heil Vaterland'. Even in dress, Schuschnigg imitated the Führer of Germany, creating a uniform out of his civilian clothes, by crossing a leather strap over his shoulder. The glasses he continued to wear contrasted oddly with the nearly martial effect. The only respect in which his imitation faltered was in his reluctance to call himself a dictator. So there existed a dictatorship without a dictator. Schuschnigg was not even big enough to be a Hitler, and remained only an imitator.

How can I describe the turmoil of my feelings during the days when the English press endlessly discussed the slavering of miserable Austria?

A mother is always selfish where her son is concerned. A small free country fell under the blow of the axe's hammer. New millions would have to talk in whispers and risk their lives, just as they were doing in Germany, just as I did under the Nazi shadow – just as my son had to whisper now if he wanted to go on living. Throughout those fearful events of catastrophic proportions I could think only in terms of my individual problem.

Now I understand what it was all about. I had been happy just to be out of Adolf's clutches, but for the fact that Pat felt he must declare his own private war on the Führer. I thought of all the millions of mothers throughout the world who would soon be watching their sons march eagerly into battle. Sons were always glad to go, mothers always reluctant to let them; and yet, even in the universal dilemma, ours had been a special case. All the other sons could wait quietly for their turn to fight, my son had to wage his war secretly. I sighed. This was the heritage I had given him.

I thought of Paula, too, wondering what her fate was, now that Adolf had annexed Austria. Much later I heard rumours about her. One story was that she was virtually a prisoner and threatening to do away with herself;

another was that she'd made up with Adolf and gone to Germany to be nearer to him. I have never been able to verify either of these two.

I found it impossible to take the burden, though Pat knew what he was doing, and would find his own way out. I could not remain quiet. I felt I had to do something.

I remember the mysterious telephone conversation I had had one day with a man named Fenton. I was sure he worked in an intelligence office. I must interrupt myself here to point out that the name Fenton is purely fictitious. I am not at liberty even today to say his name, nor that of his office, nor even the country to which it belongs.

At any rate then, this man whom I have arbitrarily named Fenton came to my mind. I decided to seek him out at the office for which I was convinced Pat was working. I was admitted at once, certainly because of my name, but when I asked about my son, the grey-haired man who had received me expressed astonishment. "But madam, why are you asking me about your son here? Did he tell you to come here?"

"No," I told him, "he said nothing, but I believe you have some connection with him."

Recognising my determination, the man looked at me seriously. "And what do you want, madam? Are you seeking to learn what your son is doing in Germany?"

"No," I replied, "I want more. I want him to come home, and I think you should do something to help him get out of Germany."

"I'm sorry, madam, I cannot help you. My advice to you is to do nothing, absolutely nothing. You might do your son the greatest injury if you say a word."

His expression convinced me that I'd come to the right place, but I didn't take his advice. Naturally he would say what he did. With him it was a question of war, with me it was the question of my son. Some instinct warned me that I must act. I showed him a few of the documents Pat had deposited in the bank and asked him if he thought them valuable. "You are in a position to know Adolf Hitler in Germany. If my son should get into difficulties, and I could go to the German embassy in London, and through them offer these documents to Adolf in exchange for my son's safety, do you think he would make a bargain with me?"

He had scarcely begun to examine the papers before he burst out, impulsively. "Wonderful! You are the only one, madam, in possession of the evidence concerning Adolf Hitler's descent and his family's origin." He looked at me shrewdly. "But why do you want to make such a trade? Have you any reason to believe your son is in danger?"

"I don't know," I evaded, "but he's in Germany. I am terrified that some situation may arise. That's why I want to know if you think they would make a bargain with me, and let my son leave Germany if I offer them these documents in exchange."

Fenton shook his head, and then I heard for the first time the expression which has now become a slogan. 'You can't do business with Hitler. He will certainly make a deal. We know him well enough for that. But it's extremely unlikely that he would keep his side of the bargain."

I tried to glean some encouragement from Fenton's parting words. "Have patience, madam. I will take it upon myself to look into this case personally. And though I can't promise anything, there is a reasonable certainty we'll soon have some word of your son."

I read the newspapers quickly, studying the most minute details about Nazi Germany. Every reported shooting and execution filled me with terror.

Months later I received a letter from Pat. I read trouble in the style of the phrases, the way the letters were formed, and the cold tone of its statement. The stamp and oversized letters on the envelope wore the censor's imprint.

Pat stated that he'd been called to the Chancellery and had been informed by his uncle that he must become a German citizen. "Naturally," he wrote, "I agreed, and I am sure that you will be glad to know this. Therefore please send me all my personal papers, and take all the necessary steps in England, for I am going to renounce my British citizenship."

When I had finished reading the letter, my first thought was to get in touch with Fenton again. He was my only advisor. I would go to see him that very day and consult him about it.

"Your son would never have written such a letter without some reason," was his comment, "though it would be merely a waste of time to try to guess what it is. I advise you to reply at once, refusing to sanction his change of citizenship. And don't, whatever you do, send him the papers he asks for."

"But what will happen?" I asked, fearful that this was just a new way of putting me off.

"Don't worry. You'll see him very soon."

Not knowing what else to do, I wrote to Pat as Fenton suggested, and then waited. A week passed. I tried to be calm, and outwardly I suppose I seemed calm, but every time the telephone or the doorbell rang I almost jumped out of my skin. I am sure the patience of my friends and relatives was sorely tried by the lack of interest I displayed the moment I recognised their voices. A hundred times I questioned the wisdom of Fenton's advice. He could give his opinion so objectively, I thought to myself, because he was in the position of a doctor advising a stranger.

Truly, it was like a message from another world, when I received a telegram saying: 'Tomorrow I shall be home, having a wonderful time.' The telegram was not from another world, only from Amsterdam. That meant Pat was safe in Holland, thank God.

Next morning Pat was home, bursting in the door as he had when a child. Having known since the day before that he was safe, my first question was how he had got out? Had Fenton been in touch with him? How had he escaped and managed?

Pat laughingly teased me about what a good conspirator I had become.

"I was so worried about you," I told him. "It seemed unbelievable that anyone could fight the Nazis from inside."

"Everyone in Germany yelled 'Heil Hitler', but you'd be surprised how much one can do. Anti-Hitlerism is as irrevocable as the black market."

As there is no longer any reason to keep silent, I can tell the details of Pat's leaving Germany. After receiving my letter he went to the Führer telling him that I had refused to send him his papers, and that he would therefore have to return to England to get them.

"But surely they would never let you do that?" I interrupted, showing off a little.

"Naturally not, but it was just to put them off the track."

Pat then went on to tell that his escape was based on the psychological thesis that the Gestapo, the world's most capable secret service organisation, would more easily detect an intricate, intellectual scheme, than one that was simple to the point of naivety. Something obvious would stand a much better chance of deceiving them, because they would find it difficult to conceive of anyone being crude. The crude plan by which Fenton hoped to upset their calculations was for Pat to purchase a railroad ticket from Berlin to Hamburg and reserve a cabin on a boat which was due to leave Hamburg in a few days. The Gestapo would of course be notified by the railroad and steamship company that Pat was about to leave for England and would probably wait for him at the railroad station, or the Hamburg pier. But Pat would never go there: at the hour the boat was scheduled to sail he would be in a private automobile on the way to the German/Dutch frontier.

"But suppose they were too smart for you?" I asked. "Suppose the Gestapo didn't wait until you got to Hamburg, or even the railroad station, but arrested you at home?"

"That was the risk," Pat agreed, "but I didn't think they would. They needed proof that I was trying to leave the country. I know the German Gestapo well. They would have tried to catch me in a fait accompli, that is to say at the boat."

"Good heavens, what a complicated business," I commented.

Pat laughed. "I'm sure you won't believe it when I tell you it was a magician – Bunny Aulden – who smuggled me out of the country, but that's the plain truth. You know, Mother, it is very difficult for agents to get into Germany, so the interested parties have had to adopt all sorts of unlikely characters to do their work. Many of them are actors or barbarians. The place of communication was the Winter

Gardens. Aulden left his car parked on the street, with visible identification papers in it. I bought my railroad ticket and reserved a cabin on the boat. I even added the realistic touch of shipping my trunk ahead. Then all I had to do was 'steal' the car and I would be on my way. Aulden wouldn't report the theft until I'd had time to cross into Holland, and no one can blame him because his car was stolen. Everything was going well, and then came the blow – my own fault. I made the mistake of paying the rent before I left my flat. It was certainly stupid of me. Half an hour later I was arrested by Schaub. You see, he'd been out of Uncle Adolf's good graces ever since he got a twenty-year-old Baden-Baden girl into trouble last year. Schaub had to marry her, but that didn't quite smooth it over with Uncle Adolf. Ever since, Schaub has been trying to get back in. Maybe he thought this was the way. Anyhow I recognised his voice the moment I realised where they were taking me, to the Alexanderplatz police station. Really, I didn't know what to do, the only man who might be able to help me was Father, but would he? I wasn't on good terms with him, so it was a little chancy looking for help in that quarter. Nevertheless, I decided to try him,

[The manuscript stops here]

REFERENCES

Introduction

Alan Cassals letter (Michael Unger 1973)

Liverpool Daily Post articles (1973)

The Memoirs of Bridget Hitler (Duckworth 1979)

Bridget Hitler: My Brother-in-law Adolf (Duckworth 1979)

Alien Personal History and Statement for the Queens County Local Alien's Board (Official records 1939)

America

Bridget Hitler: My Brother-in-law Adolf (Duckworth 1979)

Alien Personal History and Statement for the Queens County Local Alien's Board (Official records 1939)

Northern Virginia Daily article (1942)

Franklin D Roosevelt, President of the United States (FBI files 1942)

New York Herald Tribune articles (1942)

The Officer Down Memorial Page Remembers ... Special Agent Howard R Stuart-Houston (US Inland Revenue website)

Three Quiet Brothers on Long Island. *The New York Times* (April 2006)

FBI report. Subject: Brigid Elizabeth & William Patrick Hitler (1942)

Walter Langer *A Psychological Profile of Adolph Hitler: His Life and Legend* (OSS 1943)

Hans Frank: *In the Shadows of the Gallows* (1946)

New York Times articles (1939-1946)

David Gardiner: *The Last of the Hitlers* (BMM 2001)

Europe

Bridget Hitler: My Brother-in-law Adolf (Duckworth 1979)

Liverpool Daily Post articles (1973)

National-sozialistische Briefe (National-Socialist Letters) (1929)

Walter Langer *"A Psychological Profile of Adolph Hitler: His Life and Legend"*. (OSS 1943)

The Discovery Channel

Daily Express various articles (1930s)

Marc Vermeeren: *De jeugd van Adolf Hitler 1889-1985 en zijn familie en voorouders* (Soesterberg 2007)

Oliver Halmburger und Thomas Staehler: Familie Hitler. Im Schatten des Diktators. Dokumentarfilm. Unter Mitarbeit von Timothy Ryback u. Florian Beierl. München: Oliver Halmburger Loopfilm GmBH u. Mainz: (ZDF-History 2005)

James J Barnes and Patience P Barnes: *Nazis in Pre-War London 1930-1939*. Brighton: Sussex Academic Press (2005)

The Memoirs

Hugh Trevor-Roper: *The New York Review of Books* (1979)

Ian Kershaw: *Hitler 1889-1936* (Allen Lane: The Penguin Press 1998)

Beryl Bainbridge (private letters 1978 and BMM 2001)

David Gardiner: *The Last of the Hitlers* (BMM 2001)

Robert Waite: *The Psychopathic God* (Da Capo Press1993)

Walter Langer *"A Psychological Profile of Adolph Hitler: His Life and Legend"*.

Ernts Hanfstaengl: *Hitler: the Missing Years* (Eyre & Spottiswoode 1957)

Hans Frank: *In the Shadows of the Gallows*

Bridget Hitler: *My Brother-in-law Adolf* (Duckworth 1979)

Joseph Murdock Dixon: *Gregor Strasser and the organization of the Nazi Party*, 1925-32 (Stanford University 1966)

Paul Maracin: *The Night of the Long Knives. Forty-Eight Hours that Changed History* (Lyon Press 2004)